Prisons of Creativity

Sparking a discussion of the importance of creativity for the well-being of society, this book highlights and argues for the potential of those in prison to learn and exercise the skills of writing, visual arts, and music; to protect their intellectual property; and to distribute their works to the public, and the consequent benefits of their creative contribution to wider society.

Focused on the premise that a nation's well-being and competitive advantage in innovation are advanced by promoting the creative efforts of all its citizens without exclusion, including those residing in prisons, this book uses the United States as a case study to illuminate the potential among any nation's prison population to contribute to its store of creative works. Arguing that creativity should be encouraged for the benefit of all, it offers a framework for how incarcerated individuals globally could be permitted to engage in learning and undertaking skills in the expressive arts to produce works for public dissemination. Supporting this argument, it explores and analyses the Intellectual Property clause of the Constitution of the United States.

Emphasizing not just the internal but also the *external* value of creativity in prison, *Prisons of Creativity* widens and elevates the discourse concerning the institution of prison in society and its social goals. It will be of great value to anyone with an interest in arts in corrections, including educators and practitioners, professionals and policy makers within the criminal justice system, and students and scholars of criminology, criminal justice, and related areas.

John R. Whitman, Ph.D., is an educator, entrepreneur, and author, writing about innovation, intellectual property protection for underserved populations, and the social economy. He has an A.B. in philosophy from Boston University, an Ed.M. in education from Harvard University, and a doctorate in education from the University of Toronto.

"As a lifelong corrections professional and advocate for incarcerated people, I wholeheartedly endorse this text for its insightful exploration of the historical and cultural shifts in prison practices and its compelling argument for harnessing the creative potential of incarcerated individuals to benefit society."

—**Carole Cafferty**, *Corrections Superintendent (retired)*

"A unique addition to the current discourse towards an inclusive creative ecosystem and the national campaign to cultivate the many undeveloped tracts of American talent. Its thesis of personal redemption and individual dignity through artistic contribution will resonate with policy makers and social activists alike."

—**Lateef Mtima**, *Professor of Law, Howard University School of Law; Director, Institute for Intellectual Property and Social Justice*

"A sweeping account of the wasted creative potential of incarcerated persons and the resulting loss of innovation and economic benefits to society. Whitman argues for a national creative carceral policy grounded on the Constitution, which secures intellectual property rights for creators regardless of class or status. A trove of arts-in-corrections programs provides a framework to promote creativity and rehabilitation for the entire prison population, numbering more people than many nations."

—**Alma Robinson**, *Executive Director, California Lawyers for the Arts*

Prisons of Creativity

Artistic Innovation During Incarceration

John R. Whitman

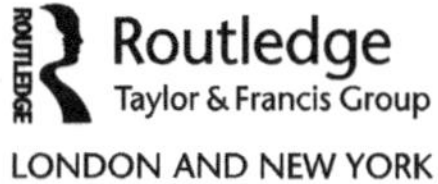

LONDON AND NEW YORK

First published 2025
by Routledge
4 Park Square, Milton Park, Abingdon, Oxon OX14 4RN

and by Routledge
605 Third Avenue, New York, NY 10158

Routledge is an imprint of the Taylor & Francis Group, an informa business

British Library Cataloguing-in-Publication Data
A catalogue record for this book is available from the British Library

ISBN: 978-1-032-90216-6 (hbk)
ISBN: 978-1-032-93477-8 (pbk)
ISBN: 978-1-003-56602-1 (ebk)

DOI: 10.4324/9781003566021

Typeset in Times New Roman
by Apex CoVantage, LLC

To all touched by the Prison Muse

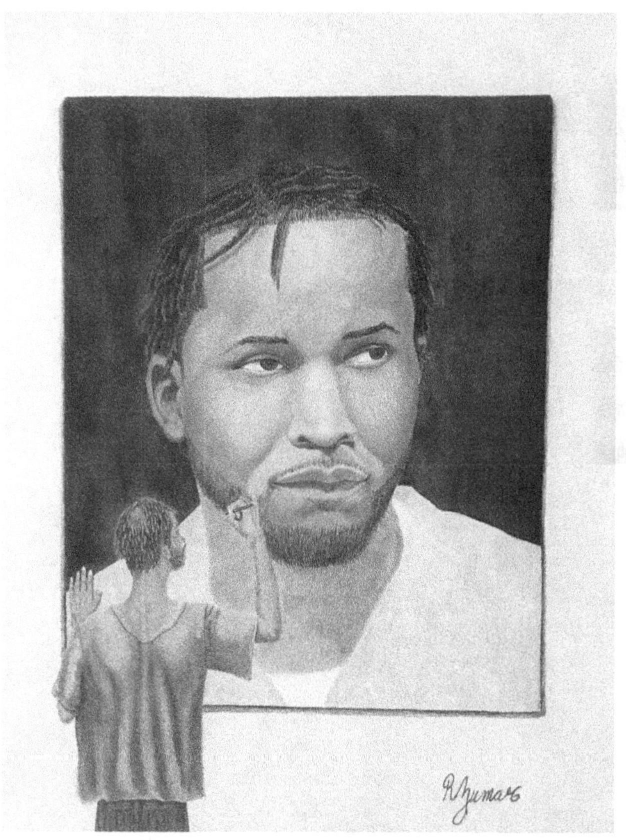

Figure 0.1 Bohemia, by R. Zumar, courtesy of the artist.

Contents

Figures

Acknowledgments

As I work as an independent researcher and writer, I owe a great debt to the many individuals who have kindly provided me with the inspiration, education, advice, and encouragement required to write this book without institutional affiliation or support. Contributions to the book include literary samples, artwork, and musical selections. My warmest thanks go to Jess Abolafia, Janet Abrams, AEmilius 7, Mark Andreason, Cedar Annenkovna, Sally-Ann Ashton, Jeanie Austin, Rayfel "Zumar" Bell, Anya Blakeley, Larry Brewster, Carole Cafferty, André de Quadros, Ava Dennis, Margaret diZerega, Elizabeth Dougherty, Nancy Eiden, Jaiquan Fayson, Malcolm Feeley, FloGriffin, Tony Graff, Eliza Granger, Bednago Harper, Grady Hillman, Brian D. Hindson, Janet (Jancy) Hoeffel, Wendy Jason, Chelsea Jordan-Makely, kidwifdacrayons, Rachel Kim, Lisa Krolak, Doran Larson, John J. Lennon, William B. Livingston III, Moira Marquis, Marcus "Da Mac" S. McKie, Chad Merrill, Viva Moffat, Esta Montano, Lateef Mtima, David Mungello, Robert Odom, Robbie Pollock, Megan Posco, David Pozen, Alma Robinson, Ashley Rubin, John Saint Amour, Victoria Scott, David Skarbek, Kyes Stevens, Heather Stuckey-Peyrot, Cuong Mike Tran, Thomas Tweh, Shaina Vanek, Robert Lee Williams, Robin Oroma Womeodu, Fury Young, Royal Young, and FREER recording artists: Michael Austin, Carl Dukes, Sedric Franklin, Cedric Johnson, Brian Lawlor, Anthony McKinney, Maxwell Melvins, Dane Newton (AKA Zealot), Valerie Seeley, Mark B. Springer, Robert Lee Williams, Naomi (Simply Naomi) Blount Wilson, and Kevin Woodley.

I am especially grateful to all the creators who participated with such enthusiasm and appreciation for someone to give their creativity attention, visibility, and respect. Permission to use their material – text and images – is thankfully received from all creators whose material is cited in the text, as well as from Lawrence Brewster, Emeritus Professor, and one anonymous contributor. Copyright to contributed materials remains with the respective authors and artists. I am also grateful for the comments of three anonymous reviewers, courtesy of the National Endowment for the Humanities, who all agreed that the book's topic was worth pursuing, despite the fact that they were also unanimous in believing the book could not be completed in time.

I also acknowledge with appreciation the role of the professional carceral community working to keep society safe, to ensure safe conditions for incarcerated people, and to be mindful of the dignity and human potential of all who are serving penal sentences. I am thankful to Routledge for publishing this work and appreciate the guidance of Morwenna Scott, commissioning editor for criminology and criminal justice, Kaustav Ghosh, senior editorial assistant for sociology and Promoth Jaikishan, assistant project manager.

Finally, my deepest appreciation is reserved for my wife, Kathryn Strickland, who has been a constant source of sunny and warm encouragement and love.

Preface

The Context

The theme of the book centers on a question that may be as old as the first human impulse to "lock 'em up": *What to do with people in prison?*

In my research, I found that the response to this question has shifted over time, reflecting different norms in different cultures influenced by different social values. The earliest known records discovered in ancient Mesopotamia indicate a rather perfunctory resolution: keep them in chains only as long as it takes to dispatch them to the next world. For millennia – that is, for about 5,000 years from the time civilization began – going to jail was but a brief and nasty waypoint on the path to the hereafter.

When the Enlightenment dawned over Europe in the 1700s, so too did the notion of lengthy incarceration as an alternative to death as punishment, for, except for capital crimes, execution was now deemed unseemly among the newly illuminated, particularly prison reformers. The lengthened time spent in prison increases the salience of questioning the social utility of incarcerated people. The officially sanctioned response in England was to stanch the growth of the prison population by transporting many elsewhere, far away, first to America and then, after the American Revolution, to Australia.

But for the most part, the response to what to do with people in prison was to put them to work, physical work, hard labor, even working them to death. The convention of appropriating the manpower of captive people has taken various forms throughout history – gladiatorial entertainment in ancient Rome, galley slavery in l'Ancien Régime, and storied Bridewell workhouses in Britain. In the United States, the record of harsh prison labor includes railroad and mining camps, convict leasing, slave-like toil on prison plantations, chain gangs, and factory work in light manufacturing, largely to meet the needs of commercial or public entities, including federal, state, and municipal government in order to eliminate or minimize the pesky cost of labor to build roads or office file cabinets. The principle of exploiting imprisoned human labor is even formally institutionalized in American carceral facilities by the Thirteenth Amendment to the U.S. Constitution, which officially sanctions "slavery" and "involuntary servitude" as punishment for those "duly convicted."

The dark record of abusive treatment of people detained in prison, particularly in the United States, is appalling and abhorrent. Deplorable treatment in private prisons operated for profit and to maximize financial returns to investors, as well as a history of slave-like exploitation of already vulnerable populations, particularly Black men in state penal institutions in the South, is well-documented (e.g., see, Alexander, 2010/2012; Bauer, 2018). And the meager compensation – well below minimum wage – offered for involuntary servitude, even in federal prisons, can be seen as an unwarranted penalty added to the punishment of serving the judicially meted out sentence of detention.

The details of the treatment of people serving time in prison are, of course, intimately known among those responsible for administrating carceral facilities, and it is not uniformly poor. But the history and extent of abuse are, perhaps, less realized by the public at large. Yet awareness is growing, as more and more of the population is tagged with a criminal record (currently 77 million Americans, or about one-third of adults) or worse, locked up. In fact, the sheer number of people currently incarcerated in the United States, recently varying between 1.7 million and 2 million souls, should demand a national public reckoning of how their time in prison is actually spent. The treatment of people in involuntary detention affects all races and ethnicities behind bars. As they all face time being incarcerated, the question of what to do with residents during incarceration is equally pertinent to all, regardless of race, ethnicity, or other characteristics.[1]

The Shift

Reflecting on how time is spent in penal institutions inspired me to propose changing the paradigm of engaging people doing prison time, shifting from a primary focus on exploiting their labor power to opening an opportunity for society itself to benefit from the creative potential of so many humans held in detention. It is well past the time for society, particularly in the United States, to reconsider and revise the practices associated with the orthodox justifications of prison as currently implemented to reduce social harm caused by crime – incapacitation, deterrence, retribution, and rehabilitation. As documented by investigative journalists Shane Bauer (2018) and Bill Keller (2022) and founder of the American Prison Writing Archive Doran Larson (2013, 2024), while there may be exceptions, none of these four goals have for the most part proven to achieve their aims *as implemented* in practice in American prisons. On the contrary, in many cases, as documented in these citations, they may have caused even greater harm to society than the crimes they address.

This shift in the paradigm of the utility of prison time, which has universal potential, is especially relevant and timely in the United States. Characteristics of social institutions, including prisons, are largely determined by culture and, as such, will vary in different countries and even across time within the same country. A few cross-cultural comparative studies have been undertaken to describe and explain differences in penal practices between the United States and a number of other counties including Anglo and Nordic nations (Pratt & Eriksson, 2013); South Africa, Germany, the Netherlands, France, Italy, Japan (Cavadino & Dignan, 2006); and Brazil, Bolivia, England, the American Civil War, and in demographically specific populations housed in women's prisons and gender nonconforming units (Skarbek, 2020).

Beginning in the 1990s, after a period of innovations in effective rehabilitation, the United States reversed course, initiating a period of relatively severe punitive practice impinging on rights beyond the loss of freedom by physical detention and notably reducing educational programing (Phelps, 2011). Some other countries, in contrast, carefully safeguard the cultural and human rights of individuals while incarcerated. Consider, for example, the so-called Nelson Mandela Rules of the United Nations, which provide standard minimum rules for treatment of incarcerated residents: that "all prisoners shall be treated with the respect due to their inherent dignity and value as human beings"; that "education, vocational training and work" should be provided; and that "recreational and cultural activities shall be provided in all prisons for the benefit of the mental and physical health of prisoners" (United Nations Office on Drugs and Crime, 2015, pp. 2, 3, 31). Note also that Norway, in particular, limits its punitive sanctions to doing time, upholding all of the individual's other rights during incarceration (Kriminalomsorgen, 2021; Ploeg, 2012, December 18).

I wrote this book to propose, therefore, that the United States could adopt at the state and federal levels a more humane justification for incarceration as: *the temporary restriction of movement while affording the opportunity for securing dignity and providing public benefit through creative expression.* This carceral goal promises both the fulfillment of the statutory sentence of time in prison to protect the safety of society and the further possibility of benefiting society through the creative output of those doing time. Moreover, the acquisition and performance by residents of the practical and life skills involved in creative expression will likely reduce tensions during imprisonment, benefiting both correctional officers and residents, and also benefit the residents themselves following eventual release. Based on my research for this book, the experience of arts-in-corrections programs, such as Rehabilitation Through the Arts (RTA) in New York prisons[2] and others, suggests to me that such a creative carceral policy is feasible and should seriously be considered for nationwide adoption.

Moreover, if residents could build financial reserves, however modest, from the sale of their creative output to better position them for community re-entry, so much the better for all. There is understandable opposition to allowing people convicted of wrongdoing to profit from their crimes. Indeed, there are cases of prisons prohibiting financial benefits from works related to one's crimes and even garnishing payments made for creative works unrelated to crimes, works that would otherwise benefit society (Alter, 2018). The content of creative works notwithstanding, categorically denying residents the opportunity to apply their creative talents while in detention serves only to discourage them from undertaking efforts that could ease both the burden of prison administration and benefit society. The opportunity cost of suppressing such creativity deserves to be considered in light of the more positive outcomes that could be attained through a creative carceral policy.

If creativity were to occupy those in prison, why would this provide value to society?

First, including incarcerated people, an appreciable number, in the overall pool of potential creators in the nation raises the overall probability of innovation. Incarcerated people have a unique perspective. They have witnessed both crime and punishment and thus have a lived experience to share with others about conditions leading to such misfortune, experiences endured as a result of society's retribution, and accounts shaped by such experiences that society could glean from no other source. Evidence for this is amply indicated by the American Prison Writing Archive (APWA)[3] and contributions to PEN America's Prison and Justice Writing Program.[4] Such accounts may well provide society with beneficial perspectives and insights not otherwise possible.

A similar logic applies to formerly enslaved people. The histories of people formerly in bondage drawn from interviews and diaries, in effect the stories of "ex-slaves," to use the terminology of the Federal Writers' Project, provide an invaluable record of the experience of bondage (Litwack, 1979). As described by Benjamin A. Botkin, the chief editor of the Writer's Unit of the Library of Congress project in 1941, such accounts constitute a folk literature and history to provide us with a unique and invaluable understanding (Botkin, 1941). As with those without a voice in bondage, people in prison also have stories to tell that could offer similar social value – not of a material or financial character, but one of an otherwise intangible historical and human essence. Legal scholar Lateef Mtima notes that while useful innovations can improve daily life, expressive works can "improve *humanity* itself" (Mtima, 2024, p. 116). The narratives told by people in prison or recently incarcerated, including R. Dwayne Betts (Betts, 2009), Piper Kerman (Kerman, 2011), and Stanley Tookie Williams (Williams, 2004), to name just a few (I cite many more in the book), and as compiled and documented by divinity scholar Kaia Stern in her book, *Voices from American Prisons* (Stern, 2014), and Doran Larson through the APWA (Larson, 2013, 2024) provide compelling examples of authentic stories recounting lived carceral experiences. But the ultimate benefit and social value of such stories will be imputed by society itself. Moreover, allowing creators to protect their intellectual property gives them an incentive to tell their stories, as I have argued elsewhere (Whitman, 2024); without such protection, why would they bother?

The Prospect

The prospect of adopting a carceral creativity policy lies at the intersection of prison and creativity:

Prison: Every nation has a prison system *to protect the safety of society*. Some nations also have prison systems at the provincial or state levels, as well as the local county or municipal levels. Prisons, including jails and other structures and mechanisms for involuntary detainment, regardless of jurisdictional division, provide the means of social control that together constitute a significant portion of a nation's carceral regime. Moreover, as penal scholar John J. DiIulio, Jr. wrote late in the twentieth century, *competent organizational leadership and management in corrections is crucial to the effective operation of prisons* (DiIulio, 1987, p. 256). His focus on the role of competent management suggests to me that I begin consideration of a new carceral creativity policy not with a policymaker's perspective, but that of a corrections superintendent.

Creativity: All prisons confine people who, regardless of political ideology, nationality, ethnicity, race, religion, sex, gender, or preferred values, share a common evolutionary membership as human beings. Citizenship rights notwithstanding – protected, suspended, or eliminated as a result of incarceration – all people in prisons share the human capacity for creativity. When such creativity gets put to use for the benefit of society, it's called innovation. And *innovation is what drives the nation's quality of life and its economic competitiveness* around the world. To argue in favor of a carceral creativity policy invites an exploration and understanding of the phenomenon of creativity itself to establish evidence of and an appreciation for its universal human relevance.

The prospect of a carceral policy to achieve the twin goals of protecting society and promoting innovation should be among the top priorities of policymakers and politicians of all ideological persuasions concerned with their nation's well-being. In the book, I try to make the case for a justified carceral policy that will unfetter the creative potential in the nation's prisons and thus add to the stock of the nation's innovation. My premise is that there is a justifiable purpose of prison consistent with ensuring public safety: *temporary physical detention and the loss of the liberty of movement for a period commensurate with the wrongdoing, while safeguarding all other human rights*. This premise provides a singular, clear, measurable, and humane justification for prison.

As to the four prevailing justifications for prison, too often, *incapacitation* is achieved through over-crowding, physical brutality, and often solitary confinement; *deterrence* of criminal behavior, both by the individual in detention and among others who would presumably refrain from unlawful behavior based on the unlikely consequences of imprisonment, has not been proven effective, for rates of recidivism are exceedingly high and prison appears to fail to much deter crime overall; *retribution* has been categorically rejected as morally repugnant since the time of the ancient Greeks; and *rehabilitation*, which can never be forcefully imposed, must be sought through the individual's own aspirations for self-improvement; and rehabilitative programs, regardless of effectiveness, have simply not been consistently available to residents.[5]

By promoting voluntary engagement in creative endeavors, justice is served through sentences of detention commensurate with the violation, *during which time the resident may voluntarily engage in creating artistic works ranging from literature to visual arts to music and more*. This would, of course, be in addition to other opportunities for vocational and practical skill-building training or higher, more theoretical and knowledge-based education, such as high school- and college-level educational courses. Such education is described in *Higher Education and the Carceral State*, edited by Annie Buckley (Buckley, 2024); other sources provide a chronology of prison education in North America (Gehring & Eggleston, 2006) and a global review of prison education (Behan, 2021).

The Book

Because of the global distribution of prisons and the universal human impulse to be creative among prison populations everywhere, this book should have global relevance. As Pope Francis, who advocates for prison reform, said to the world in reference to art created by women in a prison in Venice, it is essential that the carceral system provide residents with the means for growth and preparation for community re-entry, and that dignity could be promoted by nurturing talents otherwise thwarted by life's circumstances (Povoledo, 2024, April 28).

While the topic of creativity in prison is universal in scope, I focus on a single country, the United States, making occasional references to carceral regimes in other nations. The United States is an outlier among carceral regimes, combining a commitment in its founding declarations to secure *inalienable* natural human rights – including life, liberty, and the pursuit of happiness – yet having among the highest rates of incarceration and executions in the world. It may nevertheless serve as an instructive case in comparison to other countries to inspire a more international discourse. I look primarily at federal and state prisons, including public and private, for-profit prisons at the state level, but I will also mention county jails and houses of correction, juvenile detention centers, and other forms of detention.[6]

I offer the book to readers worldwide as a catalyst to unfetter artistic creativity during incarceration and to institutionalize creativity as a core feature of a modern, more humane carceral model. The policy change advocated here may best be achieved through constructive collaboration and mutual respect between corrections authorities and educators who, together, might influence policymakers and legislators. May such change be achieved by working within the system and ensuring that benefits to all can be obtained and appreciated.

Notes

1 I use the term "resident" throughout to indicate a person living in detention.
2 See: https://rta-arts.org/blog/unlocked/, cited 8 July 2024.
3 See: https://prisonwitness.org/, cited 12 July 2024.
4 See: https://pen.org/prison-writing/, cited 12 July 2024.
5 To learn how law schools teach the purpose of prison, consult a law textbook such as *Criminal Law*, by Kevin McMunigal (2018).
6 Being unwillingly detained but not necessarily in confinement applies to slavery and other forms of forced servitude, but this is not my main focus here (except as it appears in the Thirteenth Amendment). For those interested, Orlando Patterson provides a global sociology and history of slavery in his book, *Slavery and Social Death: A Comparative Study* (Patterson, 1982). This is a good book to read in carceral studies, for one develops an awareness of how the concepts of individual, freedom, and slavery have evolved over time and in different cultures. How, for example, might the meaning of imprisonment as punishment, or even slavery, be different at a time prior to Enlightenment notions of the individual and freedom?

References

Alexander, M. (2010/2012). *The new Jim Crow: Mass incarceration in the age of colorblindness*. The New Press.

Alter, A. (2018, February 17). A prisoner got a book deal. Now the state wants him to pay for his imprisonment. *The New York Times*. www.nytimes.com/2018/02/17/books/curtis-dawkins-graybar-hotel-prisoner-book-deal.html?searchResultPosition=1 cited 26 August 2019.

Bauer, S. (2018). *American prison: A reporter's undercover journey into the business of punishment*. Penguin Books.

Behan, C. (2021). *Education in prison: A literature review*. UNESCO Institute for Lifelong Learning.

Betts, R. D. (2009). *A question of freedom: A memoir of learning, survival, and coming of age in prison*. Penguin Group.

Botkin, B. A. (1941). *Slave narratives: A folk history of slavery in the United States from interviews with former slaves* (Federal Works Agency, Trans.). Library of Congress.

Buckley, A. (Ed.). (2024). *Higher education and the carceral state*. Routledge.

Cavadino, M., & Dignan, J. (2006). *Penal systems: A comparative approach*. Sage Publications.

DiIulio Jr., J. J. (1987). *Governing prisons: A comparative study of correctional management*. The Free Press.

Gehring, T., & Eggleston, C. (2006). *Correctional education chronology*. California State University.

Keller, B. (2022). *What's prison for? Punishment and rehabilitation in the age of mass incarceration*. Columbia Global Reports.

Kerman, P. (2011). *Orange is the new black: My year in a women's prison*. Spiegel & Grau; Random House.

Kriminalomsorgen. (2021). *Operational strategy for the Norwegian Correctional Service, 2021–2026*. Norwegian Correctional Service.

Larson, D. (Ed.). (2013). *Fourth city: Essays from the prison in America*. Michigan State University Press.

Larson, D. (2024). *Inside knowledge: Incarcerated people on the failures of the American prison*. New York University Press.

Litwack, L. F. (1979). *Been in the storm so long: The aftermath of slavery*. Vintage Books.

McMunigal, K. (2018). *Criminal law: Problems, statutes, and cases*. Carolina Academic Press.

Mtima, L. (2024). Copyright and the interdependent relationship between social utility and social justice. In S. D. Jamar & L. Mtima (Eds.), *The Cambridge handbook of intellectual property and social justice* (pp. 115–130). Cambridge University Press.

Patterson, O. (1982). *Slavery and social death: A comparative study*. Harvard University Press.

Phelps, M. S. (2011). Rehabilitation in the punitive era: The gap between rhetoric and reality in U.S. prison programs. *Law & Society Review*, *45*(1), 33–68.

Ploeg, G. (2012, December 18). Norway's prisons are doing something right. *The New York Times*. www.nytimes.com/roomfordebate/2012/12/18/prison-could-be-productive/norways-prisons-are-doing-something-right cited 8 September 2023.

Povoledo, E. (2024, April 28). Pope's visit to art exhibition in prison is a first for Venice Biennale. *The New York Times*. www.nytimes.com/2024/04/28/world/europe/venice-biennale-prison-vatican-pope.html cited 28 April 2024.

Pratt, J., & Eriksson, A. (2013). *Contrasts in punishment: An explanation of Anglophone excess and Nordic exceptionalism*. Routledge.

Skarbek, D. (2020). *The puzzle of prison order: Why life behind bars varies around the world*. Oxford University Press.

Stern, K. (2014). *Voices from American prisons: Faith, education, and healing*. Routledge.

United Nations Office on Drugs and Crime. (2015). *The United Nations standard minimum rules for the treatment of prisoners (the Nelson Mandela rules)*. Vienna International Centre, Justice Section, Division for Operations.

Whitman, J. R. (2024). Intellectual property empowerment and protection for prisoners. In S. Jamar & L. Mtima (Eds.), *Handbook of intellectual property and social justice* (pp. 245–264). Cambridge University Press. https://doi.org/10.1017/9781108697613

Williams, S. T. (2004). *Blue rage, black redemption: A memoir*. Simon & Schuster.

Introduction

The Prospect of Creativity behind Bars

Have *you* ever been in prison or jail? Or do you have an immediate family member who has ever been to prison or jail? If you are in the United States, you are hardly alone. According to the Prison Policy Initiative, 113 million adults can make the same claim, which is nearly 44% of the adult population based on the 2020 census. Indeed, the carceral landscape today is vast, both geographically and demographically. According to the Prison Policy Initiative, in 2023, there were 1.8 million people residing in 1,566 state prisons, 98 federal prisons, 3,116 local jails, 1,323 juvenile correctional facilities, 181 immigration detention facilities, and 80 Indian country jails.[1] Additionally, by the end of 2021, some 1,131 people were incarcerated in 36 military correctional facilities in the United States, the Middle East, Europe, and Asia (Field, 2022, p. 1).

And, while there are currently nearly two million people now in jail or prison in America, which is about 16% of the world's total prison population of 11 million (Fair & Walmsley, 2024, p. 2), there are 4.9 million people in America who have previously been incarcerated, 19 million people convicted of a felony, and 79 million with a criminal record.[2] That's one with a criminal record out of every four and a quarter of people in the nation's population. Now imagine if they all wore red shirts. You would see them everywhere.

If a country incarcerates a high proportion of its population, it shouldn't take long for the numbers to grow. The United States imprisons about 600,000 people per year, which adds over six million to the total every decade. The country currently imprisons 531 people per 100,000 in the population, more than every other country except American Samoa, Turkmenistan, Rwanda, Cuba, and El Salvador (Fair & Walmsley, 2024, p. 2). For the sake of comparison, Russia imprisons 300 per 100,000 of its population (that we know about); the United Kingdom, 145; Switzerland, 73; and Japan, 36.[3] If America's current prison population of some 1.8 million people were a city, it would be the fifth largest city in the nation. I call it *Prisonopolis*.

What does it cost to lock up so many people? As of this writing, the U.S. government pays $80.7 billion annually on public jails and prisons, or $241.45 per citizen, per year. But that is actually a vanishingly lowball figure. For the

DOI: 10.4324/9781003566021-1

real cost of prison to both the individual and society is far higher. Consider, for example, the lost wages of the incarcerated; the life-long lowering of income levels; inmate fees for telephone, emails, visitation, and personal consumable items; the reduction in their lifetime earnings (and foregone taxes to society); the cost of divorce; the cost to children as they suffer from the loss of a parent to prison and may themselves become homeless or turn to crime; adverse health effects and risk of higher mortality. One study estimates an aggregate cost to society of $500 billion per year or $1,500 per citizen.[4] For comparison, in fiscal year 2024, the national transportation budget was $94 billion and the defense budget was $644 billion.[5] There is no question that the financial and social cost of incarceration in our criminal justice system is staggering.

And yet there is an *additional* opportunity cost to society that hasn't been considered, much less measured. And this is what this book is about: the loss to society of the *creative potential* of people in prison. When such creativity provides a useful function, it's called *innovation.* And innovation is sought and prized by every nation on the earth. This is the prospect of creativity behind bars.

Here you will learn what is meant by creativity and why it was so important to the authors of the U.S. Constitution; what we as a society are losing by not supporting creativity among our prison population; what kinds of creativity have emerged from prisons in history and who is trying to be creative in prison right now, despite the obstacles they face. You will also be introduced to key nonprofit organizations that facilitate creativity in prison and how such organizations might collaborate to promote even greater creativity through a proposed nationwide framework for carceral creativity. What is needed, I argue, is a *national carceral creativity policy*.

To start, we need to recognize and appreciate that the job of people working in corrections is incredibly challenging.[6] They are not responsible for creating carceral policy. Instead, federal and state policies are determined by policymakers and politicians who thrust almost impossible expectations on the ability of corrections professionals to safeguard the public and also to safely control often unruly residents who have no interest in being under their control, many for years on end. Such policies variously aim to achieve the four age-old goals that justify prison: incapacitation, deterrence, retribution, and rehabilitation. These carceral goals have been challenged as ineffective and can cause extreme harm to people in prison, affecting corrections workers, and, ultimately, society. They are long overdue for critical evaluation and possibly displacement by a new carceral theory based on a modern understanding of evidence-based principles of human development, including, I argue, by engaging residents in creativity.

The approach to engaging residents in creative efforts might well make the job of corrections easier and more effective and thus strengthened. For surely, there will be no support for creativity in prison without the approval and engagement of willing correctional administrators and obliging officers.

Sociologist Michelle Phelps notes that in the Progressive Era, penitentiary administrator Donald Clemmer advocated for rehabilitation through productive use of social and leisure time over work in his landmark book, *The Prison Community* (Phelps, 2011, p. 42). Correctional professionals today who support such an approach may become the most effective witnesses to convince policymakers and politicians to support a theory of carceral creativity. According to prison scholar John DiIulio, Jr., James Bennett, who served as director of the Federal Bureau of Prisons from 1937 to 1964, believed that resident self-improvement was *essential* to humane custody (DiIulio, 1991, p. 125).

I draw from both primary and secondary sources in the book and have benefited enormously from experts in the fields of creative arts and penal systems. In addition to the bibliography, Appendix A includes recommended resources. Among my primary sources are currently incarcerated creators who signed a consent form to be interviewed via mail or email for the book in exchange for a financial honorarium. Some also provided material, including artwork, for the book in exchange for attribution and additional payment. Appendix B describes my methodology.

While I draw on examples of artistic works in various modalities, this is not intended to be an *art book*, either visually or in commentary. For an outstanding example of that genre, I highly recommend Nicole R. Fleetwood's account, *Marking Time: Art in the Age of Mass Incarceration* (Fleetwood, 2020). Dr. Fleetwood and others are far more qualified than I to proffer such a work. Nor is this an objective, dispassionate, analytical work. I wrote this book independently under the rubric of my Creative Prisons Project[7] because, based on my research, I strongly favor and advocate for creativity in prison as a matter of policy. I do not identify with the "abolish prison" movement, though I admire and cite many of those who do. In a separate work I hope to address the need instead to "abolish poverty" (Desmond, 2023), which may align with abolitionist concerns to redress certain failures of the prison industrial complex (Davis, 1995, February 20, 2003). I do hope that by the end of this book, you will share my conviction, so to speak, to promulgate a creative carceral policy. I cite my sources, but all errors, misunderstandings, and omissions remain my own.

▪ ▪ ▪

To begin, imagine for a moment that you are the warden or superintendent[8] of a prison. As superintendent, you are responsible for the *entire* operations of the facility. Regardless of the stated correctional purpose, philosophy, or ideology, your *primary* concern is twofold, one external to the prison: to protect the public; the other internal: to maintain order among the residents. What does "order" mean? To invoke John DiIulio, Jr., a long-standing penal scholar with a decade of experience with hundreds of federal, state, and local commissioners, superintendents, officers, counselors, probation and parole agents, and others involved in carceral practice, *order* means no disruption, particularly of a harmful physical nature, to the safety of others in the facility (DiIulio, 1991, p. 194).

In spite of significant odds, including inadequate funding, overcrowding, particularly aggressive gang members and mentally unstable residents, an unsupportive public, and even a critical shortage of staff, your professional ability to manage the prison is probably the most important factor determining the success of your prison. Some prisons appear to function well, while others have been shown to fail, even requiring a court-ordered consent decree, a legal agreement involving external management oversight by a federal court. Under these circumstances, how do you begin to consider engaging your residents in the creative enterprise? This is the question I address in this book.

It is not my aim to highlight carceral successes and failures, much less to prescribe how superintendents or correctional officers should do their jobs.[9] The focus of this book is on *creativity* and its value in the carceral context. Definitions of creativity abound. A useful, synthetic definition of creativity based on a content analysis of articles that explicitly define the term can be found in "Why isn't creativity more important to educational psychologists? Potentials, pitfalls, and future directions in creativity research" (Plucker et al., 2004, p. 90). For our purposes, I simplify and generalize a definition of creativity as making something that is *new* and *useful*.[10] By "useful," I mean it has some social utility, even if purely esthetic or expressive and not necessarily functional in an instrumental way. While this concise definition sounds straightforward enough, it is both massively broad in its inclusion of the range of human output that can be considered creative and also deceptively simple, for we are far from being able to explain how the human brain actually functions to produce what can be called creative.[11] And yet we know enough about the benefits of being creative to recognize the crucial role it plays for both human and national well-being.

My aim is to describe how *arts-in-corrections*, a particular form of correctional rehabilitative program that supports resident engagement in the creative arts, including writing, visual arts, music, and theater, can provide corrections administrators with an incentive for positive resident behavior resulting in improved resident relations with staff and improved behavior among themselves, thus lowering disciplinary problems and achieving one of the primary concerns of the prison superintendent. For example, public policy scholar Larry Brewster's research has shown a 66% to 81% drop in disciplinary actions and a 1.4 times benefit over costs in the early arts-in-corrections programs undertaken at the California Department of Corrections (Brewster, 1983). In a controlled study of the effects of the RTA program in New York prisons, the research found significantly reduced disciplinary infractions among residents and less time spent locked in their cells (Moller, 2011).

Regarding inter-resident behavior, as some research has shown, prison arts programs can also be effective in bridging distances and reducing tensions separating races, gangs, and other forms of in-groups and out-groups. According to one study, arts programs build important survival skills like nonviolent coping, trust, and respect (Halperin et al., 2012, p. 10). As Brewster notes, the peaceful interaction among otherwise hostile groups makes for a gratifying scene (Brewster, 2024, March 20). In some cases, such programing has resulted in higher educational achievement beyond the GED[12] while in custody as compared to a control group (Halperin et al., 2012) as well as lower rates of recidivism, which is a benefit to both society and corrections administration (Federal Bureau of Prisons, 2019, p. 19).

Arts-in-corrections, or prison arts programs,[13] have a history in the United States now spanning five decades, though not without interruption. One description of an exemplary arts-in-corrections program with roots in the 1970s is *Paths of Discovery: Art Practice and Its Impact in California Prisons*, second edition, by Larry Brewster and Peter Merts (Brewster & Merts, 2015). Arts educator Grady Hillman offers an account of his own publications since 1981 in *Arts in Corrections: Thirty Years of Annotated Publications* (Hillman, 2023). Many other professionals have been involved in providing arts in corrections around the country for decades. Indeed, for many residents in prison, incarceration has provided their first opportunity in life to learn about the arts. Yet, much more could be done.[14]

In addition to the direct administrative benefits of arts-in-corrections programing, engaging residents in the creative arts is also a way for carceral facilities to fulfill an important constitutional expectation that is not typically mentioned in the context of penology. The Constitution is usually invoked in reference to certain prisoner rights and sometimes in reference to the slavery clause in the Thirteenth Amendment. But the key clause in the Constitution that is important for purposes of creativity is called the *Intellectual Property clause* in Article I, Section 8, which reads:

> That Congress shall have Power . . . to promote the Progress of Science and useful Arts, by securing for limited Times to Authors and Inventors the exclusive Right to their respective Writings and Discoveries.

What this clause means is that creators – Authors and Inventors – can benefit financially while they exclusively own and control their creations for a limited time before such works enter the public domain, and also that the ultimate beneficiary of such creations is the United States. One publishing company, Hachette Book Group, states on the copyright page of every book it publishes, the purpose of copyright as a means to engage writers and artists to enrich culture by being creative. This protection is meant to provide an incentive for people to be creative because the fruits of their creations – their intellectual property (IP) – will yield value to the entire nation, giving it an innovative edge and helping the country to defend itself and compete globally.

The key types of IP that pertain are protected by patents and trademarks, registered by the U.S. Patent and Trademark Office, and copyrights, registered with the U.S. Copyright Office based in the Library of Congress.[15]

The authors of the Constitution did not expressly limit the Intellectual Property clause to particularly privileged groups among the population, such as educated, wealthy, or politically favored people, because they wanted the clause to be as inclusive as possible of *all* people and their human potential for creativity. As I have written elsewhere, this would include intellectual property empowerment and protection for people in prisons (Whitman, 2024). Note also that the Constitution's authors did not specify any judgmental conception of what is good or bad creativity, or good or bad uses of creativity. Novelty can be established and utility can be determined by what is needed by society, depending on the time and context.

American society has once before paid the opportunity cost of foregone creativity on a massive scale. During the era of slavery in the United States, enslaved people had no legal right to own property of any kind. Yet there is abundant evidence that they were highly creative in many culturally and socially expressive ways to benefit themselves. Because they had no recourse to own and protect their creations, they were not able to profit financially in the way intended by the Constitution. The incentive of the Intellectual Property clause therefore had no purchase as a catalyst among people in bondage to produce new and useful products to benefit anyone but themselves. We can only guess at the loss this caused to the nation during the period of slavery, for people in bondage would likely have been far *more* creative incentivized by the Intellectual Property clause of the Constitution of the United States.[16] At the time of Independence, slavery included over 20% of the nation's population, and at the time of Emancipation affected nearly four million people, or over 10% of the population.

Today, there are close to two million people in jails, prisons, and other carceral facilities, including local, state, and federal facilities. To the extent that they are unable to pursue creative work due to policies and conditions in detention while incarcerated, including the absence of any incentive, beyond earned good time, to be creative, the nation in effect similarly fails to tap into and benefit from their creative potential. To put this in perspective, this means that the population equivalent of the nation's fifth-largest city is year over year left out of the creative ecosystem so valuable to national innovation and thus, as in the time of slavery, falling short of the Constitution's promise to form a "more perfect Union."

But this need not be the case. While some prison superintendents may indeed seek to include creative arts programing in their facilities, and some already offer such programing, there is no federal or state legal obligation or normative standard to do so. Toward this end, legal scholar Avlana K. Eisenberg has written a compelling law journal article, "The Prisoner and the Polity," in which she introduces the concept of the "principle of return," the concept that limited-term punishment has an implicit but largely unrecognized obligation in the carceral sentence to prepare the resident for re-entry to society (Eisenberg, 2020, p. 4). She describes how prison programing, including educational programs for higher education as well as vocational education, which would include arts-in-corrections programs, and even religious education, should be seen as normative "practices of incarceration" contributing to preparation for re-entry (p. 5). Her paper also proposes what she calls a "communitarian approach" that would be inclusive of and benefit both residents and correctional officers (p. 10).

It is promising to see that in federal and some state facilities, the Hobby-Craft program offers an established precedent for engaging residents in creating arts and crafts, and could include more arts-in-corrections programing. Regardless of prison-sanctioned programing, the family and friends of people in detention can encourage such residents to undertake self-directed creative works and provide the materials to do so, if permitted by prison authorities. As we will see in a later chapter, there is a long history of arts in prison that provides evidence of the human impulse to create. Many residents are today active in producing a wide variety of creations, whether individually or as part of an arts-in-corrections program. A reporter in the *New York Times* has documented how Rikers Island jail in New York has been called "a literary incubator," generating many self-published books sold on the street (Kilgannon, 2024, February 18).

What, then, is my approach to arguing for a new paradigm to justify prison based on the human dignity afforded by engagement in creative work during the period of incarceration? First, for background purposes, I will recount briefly how I came to address this prospect as a result of viewing an exhibit of prison art. Then I will introduce a way to understand creativity as an innately human impulse that can build a sense of dignity. Next, I will relate how the United States came to enshrine intellectual property protection as a gift to the nation in order to promote creativity.

Turning to the carceral context, I will provide an abbreviated account of how the institution of prison evolved to become, quite unintentionally and surprisingly, a perversely ideal place for creativity to flourish. As Richard Shelton, founder of the Creative Writer's Workshop in Arizona State Prison, has noted, the undiscovered veins of creativity in prison are like the coal under West Virginia, just awaiting gratifying and life-changing discovery (Bruchac, 1984, p. xi).

Then I will provide specific evidence of how creativity has emerged from prisons historically and continues to do so. Following an account of how a small sample of currently incarcerated creators engage in their work, I will introduce you to a number of exemplary programs that facilitate arts in corrections and/or disseminate creative works to the public. As with extracted coal, the fruits of creativity must then need a means of distribution to consumers. Here I propose a nationwide framework for carceral creativity, a supply chain so to speak, that could even further benefit the nation by making a market and dissemination channel for creative products originating in the nation's 1,600-plus state and federal prisons.

Based on the foregoing elements, I contend that a national carceral creativity policy to promote arts-in-corrections programing is not only feasible but also desirable for the well-being of residents, the administration of carceral facilities, and for the nation. Undertaking the research to warrant this contention began in January 2020, in an unlikely setting in Washington, DC, where I first encountered carceral creativity.

Notes

1 See: www.prisonpolicy.org/reports/pie2023.html, cited 5 March 2024.
2 See: www.prisonpolicy.org/reports/pie2024.html, cited 8 May 2024.
3 Data compiled by the World Prison Brief at the University of London: www.prisonstudies.org/highest-to-lowest/prison_population_rate?field_region_taxonomy_tid=All, cited 14 February 2024.
4 See: https://nicic.gov/weblink/economic-burden-incarceration-us-2016, cited 14 February 2024.
5 See: https://fiscaldata.treasury.gov/americas-finance-guide/federal-spending/, cited 20 July 2024.
6 To appreciate the scope of learning to become a corrections professional, consult a textbook such as *Corrections Today* (Maroun et al., 2024).
7 My Creative Prisons Project, an unfunded, personal initiative, aims to engage more people in prison in producing creative works, to protect their intellectual property, and to facilitate ways to share their works with the public. The ultimate aim is to achieve a more perfect *and inclusive* Union by using creativity to humanize prisons and society and to promote the eradication of poverty and racism.
8 I am referring to the individual in charge of a detention facility. Warden is favored in some areas, but I will use the term superintendent throughout.
9 For many excellent insights into the improvement of prisons, please consult Bill Keller's highly informed account, *What's Prison For?* (Keller, 2022). Note also long overdue oversight legislation governing the Federal Bureau of Prisons (Davidson, 2024, July 19).
10 For those with expertise in intellectual property (IP) law in the United States: I intentionally use an expansive understanding of the term *creativity* here in reference to the arts that is inclusive of the more technical and contrasting meanings of the term in both patent and copyright law. In *patent* law, creativity is described in an instrumental sense in U.S. Code Title 35, "Patents," Section 101: "Whoever invents or discovers any new and useful process, machine, manufacture, or composition of matter, or any new and useful improvement thereof, may obtain a patent therefor, subject to the conditions and requirements of this title"; in Section 102, which describes "novelty"; and in Section 103, which describes the additional requirement of being "non-obvious." In *copyright* law, expressive creativity is treated in U.S. Code 17, "Copyrights," Section 101 as: "A work is 'created' when it is fixed in a copy or phonorecord for the

first time; where a work is prepared over a period of time, the portion of it that has been fixed at any particular time constitutes the work as of that time, and where the work has been prepared in different versions, each version constitutes a separate work"; and Section 102, which reads in part, "Copyright protection subsists, in accordance with this title, in original works of authorship fixed in any tangible medium of expression, now known or later developed, from which they can be perceived, reproduced, or otherwise communicated, either directly or with the aid of a machine or device," followed by categories of protected works. A section on historical and revision notes provides further clarification: "The two fundamental criteria of copyright protection – originality and fixation in tangible form are restated in the first sentence of this cornerstone provision. The phrase 'original works or authorship,' which is purposely left undefined, is intended to incorporate without change the standard of originality established by the courts under the present copyright statute. This standard does not include requirements of novelty, ingenuity, or esthetic merit, and there is no intention to enlarge the standard of copyright protection to require them."

11 Biologist Edward O. Wilson wrote that the universality of creativity is probably due to human behavior during the first 90% of human evolution (Wilson, 2017, p. 85).

12 General Educational Development (GED) is a measure of academic knowledge equivalent to that achieved in high school.

13 I will adopt the former to focus on corrections rather than prisons.

14 While I focus on artistic expression in this book, a case might also be made elsewhere for engaging people in prison in creating inventions through, say, maker spaces (www.makerspaces.com/what-is-a-makerspace/). Advances in lock security, shower valves, and tattoo technology have originated in prisons.

15 Technically, federal trademark protection is rooted in the Commerce Clause, Article I, Section 8, Clause 3 of the Constitution of the United States.

16 There is speculation that the cotton gin had origins in the ideas of enslaved people: www.archives.gov/education/lessons/cotton-gin-patent, cited 27 June 2024.

References

Brewster, L. (2024, March 20). Personal communication.

Brewster, L. G. (1983). *An evaluation of the arts-in-corrections program of the California Department of Corrections*. William James Association. www.ojp.gov/ncjrs/virtual-library/abstracts/evaluation-arts-corrections-program-california-department cited 20 March 2024.

Brewster, L. G., & Merts, P. (2015). *Paths of discovery: Art practice and its impact in California prisons* (2nd ed.). Self Published.

Bruchac, J. (Ed.). (1984). *The light from another country: Poetry from American prisons*. The Greenfield Review Press.

Davidson, J. (2024, July 19). Congress passes bill to impose strict scrutiny on embattled prison agency. *The Washington Post*. www.washingtonpost.

com/politics/2024/07/19/congress-bureau-of-federal-prisons-oversight-bill/ cited 20 July 2024.

Davis, A. Y. (2003). *Are prisons obsolete?* Seven Stories Press.

Davis, M. (1995, February 20). Hell factories in the field: A prison-industrial complex. *The Nation*, 229–234.

Desmond, M. (2023). *Poverty, by America*. Crown.

DiIulio Jr., J. J. (1991). *No escape: The future of American corrections*. Basic Books.

Eisenberg, A. K. (2020). The prisoner and the polity. *New York University Law Review*, *95*, 1–74.

Fair, H., & Walmsley, R. (2024). *World prison population list* (14th ed.). www.prisonstudies.org/sites/default/files/resources/downloads/world_prison_population_list_14th_edition.pdf cited 12 July 2024.

Federal Bureau of Prisons. (2019). *Legal resource guide to the Federal Bureau of Prisons 2019*. U.S. Department of Justice, Federal Bureau of Prisons. www.bop.gov/resources/pdfs/legal_guide_march_2019.pdf cited 27 September 2023.

Field, E. (2022). *Military correctional facilities: Consistent application of standards and improved oversight could enhance health and safety* (Vol. GAO-23-105082). United States Government Accountability Office.

Fleetwood, N. R. (2020). *Marking time: Art in the age of mass incarceration*. Harvard University Press.

Halperin, R., Kessler, S., & Braunschweiger, D. (2012). Rehabilitation through the arts: Impact on participants' engagement in educational programs. *The Journal of Correctional Education*, *63*(1), 6–23.

Hillman, G. (2023). *Arts in corrections: Thirty years of annotated publications*. Routledge.

Keller, B. (2022). *What's prison for? Punishment and rehabilitation in the age of mass incarceration*. Columbia Global Reports.

Kilgannon, C. (2024, February 18). How a notorious jail became a literary hotbed. *The New York Times*. www.nytimes.com/2024/02/18/nyregion/rikers-island-authors.html cited 18 February 2024.

Maroun, R. R., Siegel, L. J., & Bartollas, C. (2024). *Corrections today*. Cengage.

Moller, L. (2011). Project slam: Rehabilitation through theatre at Sing Sing Correrctional Facility. *The International Journal of the Arts in Society*, *5*(5), 9–29.

Phelps, M. S. (2011). Rehabilitation in the punitive era: The gap between rhetoric and reality in U.S. prison programs. *Law & Society Review*, *45*(1), 33–68.

Plucker, J. A., Beghetto, R. A., & Dow, G. T. (2004). Why isn't creativity more important to educational psychologists? Potentials, pitfalls, and future directions in creativity research. *Educational Psychologist*, *39*(2), 83–96.

Whitman, J. R. (2024). Intellectual property empowerment and protection for prisoners. In S. Jamar & L. Mtima (Eds.), *Handbook of intellectual property and social justice* (pp. 245–264). Cambridge University Press. https://doi.org/10.1017/9781108697613

Wilson, E. O. (2017). *The origins of creativity*. Liveright Publishing Corporation.

1 The Creative Impulse at Lincoln's Cottage

Just over three and a half miles to the northeast of the White House sits an attractive and sunny 12-room white cottage with light brown gingerbread along the rake of its gabled roof. This is where, the Civil War raging to the South, President Abraham Lincoln would retreat during the summer on horseback from the White House to find peace, quiet, and a contemplative space conducive to writing the Emancipation Proclamation in mid-1862. Walt Whitman, who lived nearby, described Lincoln's "Old Abe" as "an easygoing grey horse" carrying Lincoln "dressed in plain black, somewhat rusty and dusty" and crowned with his signature black, stovepipe hat.[1]

Today, the historic site, once known as the Soldiers' Home because it housed old and injured soldiers and now called Lincoln's Cottage, includes a museum with events for the public that have entertained nearly 340,000 visitors since 2008.[2] The museum also allows private events and in 2020 featured an exhibition of artwork by people in prison organized by the Justice Arts Coalition (JAC). The Cottage came alive with two floors of rooms filled with paintings, watercolors, drawings, and sculptures created by people behind bars.

Wendy Jason, founder and director of JAC, had invited me to visit the exhibit after we discussed my possible interest in protecting the intellectual property of incarcerated creators. She and I share a devotion to social justice. Her conviction is expressed through tireless efforts to advocate for creators in prison and to bring their art to the public, which has endeared her to a large and growing group of fans, both inside and outside prisons across the country; mine is through endeavors to protect the intellectual property of people living in underserved communities, to encourage even greater creativity within such communities, and to facilitate ways to bring creations to the public as a way to further enrich society.[3] To me, there is vast potential for creativity among underserved groups that I characterize as "dark IP," waiting to be discovered.

This exhibition was where I acquired my first artwork created by people in detention: Rayfel "Zumar" Bell's "Bohemia," a self-portrait of the earnest artist painting a new version of himself as a healthy, reformed individual, which turns out to be one of the central themes of this book; Will Livingston,

DOI: 10.4324/9781003566021-2

III's "Howlin' Wolf," depicting the rapturous blues guitarist performing at a concert; Chad Merrill's *Alfred Hitchcock*, a portrait of the movie producer looking smug with blackbirds emerging, as if in birth, from his head; and Thomas Tweh's "The Pharaoh OBAMA," a stunning facial portrait of Barack Obama as an Egyptian sovereign, done in ink.

Interestingly, before coming to America, Thomas Tweh was a native of Monrovia, Liberia. This is a country that began as a part of West Africa selected by the American Colonization Society to serve as a place for free Blacks to voluntarily relocate beginning in 1822. The Society felt this would conveniently remove the strain felt by white people of contending with a "race" they considered inferior to theirs. As told by historian Leon Litwack, in his book, *North of Slavery*, the Society's leadership thought it preferable to keep "Negroes" in a state of ignorant degradation, for they could never achieve white privilege (Litwack, 1961, p. 23). It would be more sensible and desirable, the Society reasoned, to colonize Blacks elsewhere. Litwack describes the society's sentiment in condescending reference to the "American Negro's" constitutional suitability to the fierce sun of Africa in contrast to the enjoyment of white people in the United States relieved by the eventual elimination of slavery and prejudice (p. 23).

Abolitionists would decry the movement for colonization after 1831, but in the 1850s, the removal solution would be reprised with support from the Republican party and Abraham Lincoln. In 1847, Black settlers from America had declared independence for the nation of Liberia, cementing America's position as a colonial power long before its colonization of the Philippines and Puerto Rico as a result of the Spanish-American War. So I felt it somewhat ironic to find a creation, done by a native of Liberia, for sale in Lincoln's Cottage, featuring a president who had first favored colonization, and then led a war for emancipation. The promise of redemption hung in the air at that exhibition.

Acquiring a piece of art makes one inquisitive about the artist, and so each one shared his backstory with me. I thus came to appreciate the profound truth of Bryan Stevenson's assertion in his revelatory and inspiring book about the unjust and unmerciful hardships experienced by too many people in prison, *Just Mercy*, that "*Each of us is more than the worst thing we've ever done*" (Stevenson, 2014, pp. 17–18, emphasis in original).

Viewing and purchasing what I considered art worth owning deepened my curiosity about creativity in prison and launched me on the path to write this book. To prepare for writing this story, I first wanted to learn more about creativity, the origins of the Intellectual Property clause of the Constitution of the United States, and how the prison came to be a modern institution, surprisingly enough, well-suited for developing creative talent. Let's turn to what I found.

▪ ▪ ▪

Starting with creativity, the verb "to create" has different meanings, some of which have to do with production but nothing to do with creativity as intended in this book. For example, by ignoring the warnings, he "created" trouble for himself. By assembling the pieces of a model airplane, she "created" another addition to her collection. Even "creating" a list of telephone numbers ordered alphabetically by the last name of the telephone customer would not be eligible for copyright protection as an original creation because it is a compilation of facts and not the author's original work. To use the imagination to produce something novel and useful makes much more sense in defining creativity. It is this type of creation that, when put into a form of use to others, is what we call *innovation*. The value of creativity and innovation to the nation was clearly understood by the authors of the Constitution and continues to be broadly affirmed among contemporary researchers in business and neuroscience alike.

Numerous sources have asserted the crucial value of creative thinking over the last 30 years, noting its contribution as the "quintessence of our humanity" (Dietrich, 2019, p. 36); the "defining trait of our species" (Wilson, 2017, p. 3); essential to our success in war and economics (Heilman, 2016, p. 285);[4] ensuring individual and societal adaptive capacity (Zaidel, 2014, p. 1); key to civilized progress (Hennessey & Amabile, 2010, p. 570); essential to innovation and entrepreneurship in organizations and business (Runco, 2004, p. 659); and vital to corporate survival in fast-changing markets (Amabile, 1988, p. 124).

Behavioral research provides a useful approach to defining conditions conducive to creativity in a way that can be empirically tested. In particular, psychologist Carl Rogers, best known for his approach to client-centered therapy, formulated propositions for a theory of creativity that may have some specific implications for creativity in prisons. Rogers' definition of the creative process, both artistically and technically, is consistent with our working definition of creativity – making something that is new and useful – a process arising from the "uniqueness of the individual" and the "materials, events, people, or circumstances" at hand (Rogers, 1954, p. 251).

What Rogers brings to the definition is a description of the creative *process*, which acknowledges both the individual's innate uniqueness and the individual's external environment, including "materials, events, people, or circumstances." Rogers also explains the motivation for creativity to "enhance the self" (p. 251). It makes sense to encourage people once in prison to strive to develop their productive talents, especially as the overwhelming majority will return to the community. Despite possibly different talents for creativity, Rogers believes that the urge to be creative "exists in every individual, and awaits only the proper conditions to be released and expressed" (p. 252).

What are these proper conditions? To begin, Rogers describes three that are *intrinsic* to a creative individual. *First, openness to experience*: that the creator must be able to experience stimulation without its being distorted (p. 254). *Second, an internal locus of evaluation*: that the value of the creator's product is determined internally by the creator, not externally by others. *Third, the ability to consider multiple elements and concepts*, such as "ideas, colors, shapes, relationships" and to combine and recombine them in a "new and significant way" (p. 255).

These three intrinsic conditions cannot be forced, but they can be fostered or encouraged and permitted to emerge in an arts-in-corrections program. While some people may have a greater intrinsic talent for certain creative expression, whether art, music, or mathematics, others can learn the skills of such expression, either through individual study or in classes. The implication for prisons would be to offer resources and a venue that could stimulate intrinsic talent as well as educational programs that can teach creative skills.

There are also *extrinsic* conditions to be considered by those concerned with encouraging the best climate conducive to creativity. Based on his experience in psychotherapy, Rogers believed that by ensuring psychological *safety* and *freedom*, creativity is most likely to emerge. By psychological safety, he means:

1. *Accepting the unconditional worth of an individual*; "no matter what his present condition or behavior, he is fostering creativity" (p. 257). This is the stance toward residents to be taken by an arts-in-corrections facilitator who sees the worth of a resident in terms of his or her potential, and is not prejudiced by the resident's prior behavior or current condition.
2. *Providing a climate in which external evaluation is absent*; a situation in which one is not being evaluated by an external standard of good or bad (p. 257). By this, Rogers is referring to judgments, not simply reactions. For someone to react to the creator by saying, "I don't like your work" is not to say it is good or bad, which would be an evaluation of judgment, but is a reaction based on personal preferences. Consistent with the internalized conditions noted earlier, the locus of evaluation must be determined by the creator, not by others, and if a creative work of visual art, for example, does not meet an external standard established by, say, Rembrandt or Picasso, it should be considered no less creative. In the carceral context, this condition must, of course, be qualified by what is and is not allowed within a particular prison, and correctional officers should enforce such rules accordingly.
3. *Understanding empathetically*. This means accepting an individual in the context of his or her condition. According to Rogers, it is essential to understand empathetically, sharing the viewpoint of and accepting the individual (p. 258). This also speaks to the stance of the arts-in-corrections facilitator, understanding a resident's feelings about his or her condition from the resident's viewpoint, and seeing, acknowledging, and still accepting the worth of the individual.

Turning to psychological freedom, Rogers calls for permitting a person's complete freedom of *symbolic* expression. This does not mean behavioral or physical freedom, but freedom to think, feel, and express whatever is in mind in symbolic form. Rogers also notes that with permission to be free comes responsibility to be oneself in order to achieve a secure inner sense of self-evaluation (p. 258). While a prison would certainly have limits to allowed behaviors, it will also have limits on certain symbolic representations, forbidding, for example, those associated with gangs, sex, escape, and so forth.

Rogers proposes that if the inner conditions of constructive creativity and the conditions of psychological safety and freedom are provided to a group, say an arts-in-corrections class, then, compared to a control group that does not share such conditions, this group will produce more creative products, they will be more significantly novel, and there will be more effective and harmonious interpersonal relationships in the group. He also notes that these outcomes can be measured. They could likely be measured in a prison environment.

Perhaps we can go beyond Rogers in two respects, also internal and external. By internal, I mean that the creator must first willfully commit to the creative process. Not everyone might be so inclined. I'm reminded of this light bulb joke: "How many psychiatrists does it take to change a light bulb?" The answer is, "Just one, but the bulb has to *really* want to change." A similar challenge to opting in has been reported in efforts to engage incarcerated residents in art therapy programs as a means to construct a new definition of themselves, beginning with overcoming "self-deflating and rigid defenses" (Gussak et al., 2023, p. 101).

With respect to external, we suggest additional conditions to foster creativity and likely enhance the ability of any individual in society to develop his or her intrinsic capabilities. For starters, having access to high-quality education beginning in preschool; working in an environment in which creativity and innovation are encouraged and supported rather than discouraged and smothered; being among others who share an interest in creativity and innovation rather than disparaging it; having access to materials and resources to draw on during the exploratory process; being knowledgeable about intellectual property protection and how to protect one's creative expressions; being able to litigate against those who try to misappropriate one's creative work. These are all conditions that go well beyond Rogers' enumeration, but are certainly consistent with "the materials, events, people, or circumstances" he states are important to the creative process (Rogers, 1954, p. 251).

While some residents in detention may indeed have been privileged to experience such conditions, many, particularly from economically underserved communities, have not. It should not be surprising, therefore, to see that despite the internal capacity for creation among individuals, the quality and quantity of creative output among people in limited circumstances would be vastly different from those in the population who did enjoy such cultivating conditions.

I should also note that some research has attempted to correlate creativity to intelligence as well as to personality traits (Barron & Harrington, 1981; Jauk et al., 2013). Such research may have relevance to a standard of creativity necessary in certain situations like competitive economic or academic performance; however, such correlations, valid or not, have no relevance with respect to engaging people in prison in creative enterprise. Regardless of socioeconomic background or innate qualities, the social value of any creative output will be ascertained simply by the creator's own standards or by public demand.

In short, we can safely say that despite not yet having much of an understanding of how creativity works in the brain or how it has evolved, we do know how to provide conditions likely to induce creative work in ways that can be tested and measured. Moreover, if we want to be creative, we could test if such conditions can be adapted to meet the special requirements of carceral facilities and also provide administrative benefits. Accounts by Larry Brewster and Peter Merts in the second edition of their book, *Paths of Discovery: Art Practice and Its Impact in California Prisons* (2015), appear to provide evidence of all of the elements of Rogers' theory of creativity and also demonstrate the value of arts-in-corrections programs to prison administrators.

The creative impulse, then, appears to be a capacity inherent in all of us. For some, it comes naturally; for others, the right conditions, encouragement, and instruction can help. But the social and economic importance of protecting this impulse cannot be overstated. And this is why the Constitution of the United States, written at the nation's birth, addresses the protection of creativity right alongside the ability to declare war and to make laws.

Notes

1 See: https://en.wikipedia.org/wiki/President_Lincoln%27s_Cottage_at_the_Soldiers%27_Home and www.mrlincolnswhitehouse.org/washington/homes/homes-soldiers-home/, cited 8 February 2024.
2 See: www.lincolncottage.org/, cited 15 February 2024.
3 In 2011, I had co-founded the Museum for Black Innovation and Entrepreneurship in Washington, DC to catalyze creativity to build wealth in communities like those in Southeast DC (https://mbiedc.org/).
4 Applying creativity to the instruments of war has its corollary in prisons, evidenced by the clever creation out of melted black garbage bags of a deadly shank used in a prison riot at California's Calipatria State Prison (Davis, 1995, February 20, p. 230).

References

Amabile, T. M. (1988). A model of creativity and innovation in organizations. *Research in Organizational Behavior*, *10*, 123–167.

Barron, F., & Harrington, D. M. (1981). Creativity, intelligence, and personality. *Annual Review of Psychology*, *32*, 439–476.

Brewster, L., & Merts, P. (2015). *Paths of discovery: Art practice and its impact in California prisons* (2nd ed.). Self Published.

Davis, M. (1995, February 20). Hell factories in the field: A prison-industrial complex. *The Nation*, 229–234.

Dietrich, A. (2019). Where in the brain is creativity: A brief account of a wild-goose chase. *Current Opinion on Behavioral Sciences*, *27*, 36–39.

Gussak, D. E., Odom, E., & Soape, E. (2023). Interacting through art to re-empower inmates in constructing new self-appraisals. In E. Bos & E. Huss (Eds.), *Using art for social transformation: International perspective for social workers, community workers and art therapists* (pp. 94–106). Routledge. https://doi.org/10.4324/9781003105350-8

Heilman, K. M. (2016). Possible brain mechanisms of creativity. *Archives of Clinical Neurpsychology*, *31*, 285–296.

Hennessey, B. A., & Amabile, T. M. (2010). Creativity. *Annual Review of Psychology*, *61*, 569–598.

Jauk, E., Benedek, M., Beate, D., & Neubauer, A. C. (2013). The relationship between intelligence and creativity: New support for the threshold hypothesis by means of empirical breakpoint detection. *Intelligence*, *41*, 212–221.

Litwack, L. F. (1961). *North of slavery: The Negro in the free states, 1790–1860*. The University of Chicago Press.

Rogers, C. R. (1954). Toward a theory of creativity. *EDC: A Review of General Semantics*, *11*(4), 249–260.

Runco, M. A. (2004). Creativity. *Annual Review of Psychology*, *55*(2014), 657–687.

Stevenson, B. (2014). *Just mercy*. Spiegel & Grau.

Wilson, E. O. (2017). *The origins of creativity*. Liveright Publishing Corporation.

Zaidel, D. W. (2014). Creativity, brain, and art: Biological and neurological considerations. *Frontiers in Human Neuroscience*, *8*(Article 389), 1–9.

2 The Gift of IP Protection

Given the strategic importance of innovation to a nation's competitive standing, it may seem obvious today that a nation would want to embed an imperative for creativity in its constitutional DNA. Creativity leads to the innovation necessary for national defense as well as for social and economic well-being in highly competitive global markets. In 2021, all industries related to copyright material alone contributed nearly $3 trillion, or 12.52%, to the U.S. economy (Stoner & Dutra, 2022). When copyright is combined with other IP, including utility patents, design patents, and trademarks, IP-intensive industries contributed $7.86 trillion to the economy in 2019, and together, all IP-intensive industries included 63 million jobs, about 44% of total employment in 2019 (Toole et al., 2022). Creativity, in other words, is essential to a strong nation, and everyone, without exception, should be encouraged to contribute to the country's creative strength. Indeed, from the birth of the new republic, the intent of the Intellectual Property clause in the Constitution of the United States has required that the protection of creativity by authors and inventors be equally accessible to all in America. This gift of intellectual property protection belongs to everyone. Here I explore what this assertion and its inclusivity means, particularly for those in prison.

To begin, consider what is construed as *intellectual property*. The global marketplace, including the United States, recognizes four types of creative works that are considered intellectual property: trade secrets, patents, trademarks, and copyrights (Mtima, 2015). Additionally, according to intellectual property law professor Lateef Mtima, a number of countries, including the United States, also recognize a fifth right, the right of publicity or personality rights. The World Intellectual Property Organization (WIPO), a United Nations entity based in Geneva, Switzerland, with 193 member states, serves as a global forum for IP matters.[1]

A *trade secret* is simply any valuable information that offers a competitive advantage and is kept secret from the public in order to retain this advantage. This might include the secret formula for making Coca-Cola, protected software that controls a piece of machinery, or a confidential mailing list of customers. Trade secrets, as intellectual property, are protected from theft, but

DOI: 10.4324/9781003566021-3

by their confidential nature are not registered with any outside entity such as the government. If by accident, or otherwise, the trade secret becomes known to the public, protection is lost forever.

A *patent* protects inventions that create something useful, new, and non-obvious. The design of the invention is sent to the U.S. Patent and Trademark Office for review by qualified patent examiners to determine its eligibility for either design or utility patent protection. If approved, such protection lasts 20 years from the filing date.

A *trademark*, which can also be a service mark, is one or a few words, a symbol, color, design, sound, or combination used to uniquely and distinctively identify the source of the relevant goods or services. The aim of a trademark is to avoid consumer confusion in associating a particular product or service with the individual or firm that offers it. Trademark applications for protection are sent to the U.S. Patent and Trademark Office, where they are reviewed for eligibility. If approved for registration, the trademark symbol, ™, or sales mark symbol, ℠, may be replaced by the registered trademark symbol, ®. Trademark protection has no time limit, but requires renewal every ten years.

A *copyright* protects original, creative, expressions fixed in a tangible medium, such as paper, canvas, film, or sculpture. A copyright application, such as for a poem, book, and photograph, is submitted to the U.S. Copyright Office for review.[2] If it meets the requirements for protection, the copyright holder may file an infringement claim against a party who misappropriates the owner's rights in federal court or with the Copyright Claims Board of the U.S. Copyright Office. There are some exceptions that allow *fair use*, such as for non-commercial, nonprofit educational purposes. The copyright symbol is ©. Copyright protection lasts the length of the author's life plus 70 years.

Because copyright is the principal form of intellectual property protection highlighted in this book, it is worth clarifying the purpose of copyright as illuminated by a former Register of Copyrights, Abraham Kaminstein, testifying before the Senate:[3]

> The basic purpose of copyright protection is the public interest, to make sure that the wellsprings of creation do not dry up through lack of incentive, and to provide an alternative to the evils of an authorship dependent upon private or public patronage. As the founders of this country were wise enough to see, the most important elements of any civilization include its independent creators – its authors, composers, and artists – who create as a matter of personal initiative and spontaneous expression rather than as a result of patronage or subsidy. A strong, practical copyright law is the only assurance we have that this creative activity will continue.

Publicity rights refer to an individual's right to prevent others from using his or her name, image, or other recognizable features for commercial purposes without permission. An example might be the use of a popular sports player's likeness in a video game. Like trade secrets, the protection of such rights is not registered with a government agency. In cases of dispute, a judge will be required to sort out competing rights, such as First Amendment rights versus an individual's claim to protect his or her personal features from commercial exploitation by others. Resolution to such disputes is not always straightforward. Depending on the state, post-mortem publicity rights can last for decades.

Intellectual property is a key part of modern economies driven by innovation. What concerns us in this book is whether everyone, including people in prison, is effectively able to protect their intellectual property. What *is* clear is that the Constitution intended to extend such protection to everyone, without exclusion (though until the Thirteenth Amendment, ratified in 1865, 78 years after the Constitution was written, this did not apply to people in slavery).

Given the enormity of the task of writing a constitution for a new nation, it is something of a miracle that the authors of the Constitution had the foresight to build federal protection of intellectual property into the Constitution along with matters like the structure of government, elections, taxes, and the currency. The Articles of Confederation, which preceded the Constitution, made reference to retaining states' rights, and 12 of the 13 states had some legislation for IP protection, but there was no unifying protection for the nation until the Constitution. To understand what was most important to the constitutional authors, and why they wrote the Constitution as they did, we need to know a bit about what the world was like in their era and how they thought they could build national strength beyond a collaborative military defense. Remember, when the Constitution was penned in 1787, there had never in human history been a democracy quite like the one the founders established. Once we know a bit more about what the founders knew at the time, the reasons for why the document includes the Intellectual Property clause should become clear.

We begin with the Declaration of Independence, dated July 4, 1776. In this masterfully worded proclamation, the 56 signatories, designating themselves as the representatives of the United States, in effect filed a declaration of divorce from the King of England, stating "that they are absolved from all Allegiance to the British Crown, and that all political connection between them and the State of Great Britain, is and ought to be totally dissolved." Now, the new country would have to craft its own laws.

The shooting had commenced over a year earlier, on April 19, 1775. Enough was enough with the tyranny of the monarchy! Two years after the Declaration, on July 9, 1778, the 13 original states signed the Articles of Confederation. This confederacy affirmed the sovereignty of each, separate state, but also bound them together for purposes of a common defense, clearly a matter of survival under the circumstances of military hostility by England. Battles would continue until British General Cornwallis surrendered at Yorktown in October 1781. But the Revolutionary War was not officially over until the Treaty of Paris was signed on September 3, 1783, eight long years after the first shots were exchanged in the now historic communities of Concord and Lexington, Massachusetts.

With England temporarily out of the way (at least until the war of 1812), the founders could reflect and debate on what manner of nation they had brought forth. As a confederacy, each state, fearful of the potential despotism of a centrally controlled government like the monarchy they just overthrew, tenaciously retained its own sovereignty. This is akin to a couple agreeing to date, but far from willing to get married (Article III of the Articles of Confederation calls it "a firm league of friendship"). Still, some of the new leaders were deeply worried about the vulnerability of such a contingent relationship. They reasoned that an even stronger mutual commitment, particularly to secure a unified national defense against far more powerful nations like England, France, and Spain, was absolutely necessary. They argued for a new and robust compact as a formidable *union*, stronger together, a relationship more like a marriage than a league of friendship.

With steely commitments to their independence and a fearsome allergy against any monolithic central control, with or without a crown, the union was difficult for the states to arrange. The compromise necessary to achieve unity was to strike a balance of power between a federal locus of limited national control and individual state's rights. They retained from the Articles of Confederation the modest term "president" to address the chief executive of their proposed union. But southern states would not even think of joining a union unless they could keep their slave societies, an institution diametrically at odds with the very principles of the natural rights pronounced in the Declaration of Independence.

Yet, compromise was achieved and the union was formed. The legal document sealing this union has rightly been labeled by historian David Waldstreicher as *Slavery's Constitution*, and in this book, he notes that while slavery is never mentioned in the Constitution, of some 84 clauses in the document, six concern slaves and their owners and more have implications for slavery (Waldstreicher, 2019, p. 3). At the end of a process of multiple revisions, the Constitution, signed on September 17, 1787, declared the aim "to form a more perfect Union" – perhaps not *the* perfect Union quite yet, but a collectively affirmed aspiration toward that end. The Bill of Rights soon followed, ratified four years later, on December 15, 1791.

One lesson from the era of the constitutional authors is that a deep mistrust of strong, central governance, particularly among the Southern states, could be balanced by the benefits of unified states retaining control of most of their separate interests. In fact, the compromises in the Constitution continue to challenge our democracy in profound ways, particularly those directly tied to southern interests in protecting slavery and the way of life made possible by free labor. These links to slavery are revealed and explained in the essays that appear in *The 1619 Project* (Hannah-Jones et al., 2021), which provide historical accounts of how those in bondage directly contributed to our institutions, traditions, music, art, literature, and conception of democracy (p. xxxii).

One way states could be stronger together was to protect certain individual rights throughout all states. These rights are most prominently, if sometimes ambiguously, expressed in the Bill of Rights, the first ten amendments to the U.S. Constitution. Several years before the Bill of Rights was adopted in 1791, at the Constitutional Convention of 1787, there was one other legal right pertaining to individuals that was deemed so important to the authors that it appears in the very *first* article of the Constitution itself. Surprisingly few people are aware of how the Constitution directs Congress to protect an individual's ownership of his or her intellectual property.

The idea of protecting intellectual property was not new in the mid-1700s. The British claim the world's first copyright law in the Statute of Anne of 1710, but some suggest that Venice, Italy, issued what may be the first known example of a copyright around the time Columbus arrived in the New World, over 200 years earlier. This account begins with Johannes Gutenberg, who is credited with inventing the modern printing press in Germany around 1440. But he had no patent protection and lawsuits left him relatively poor at his death. His printing press found its way to Venice shortly after its invention. With its strategic access to commercial routes to most of the known world, Venice soon became a hotbed of publishing. But along with the ability to print literature in volume came the ease of copying it without permission. This created a threat to the ownership of originality. So, the Venetians, with their preternatural commercial wisdom, may have been the first to invent the construct of copyright by granting official publishing privileges in the 15th century (Lane, 1973, p. 311). In the period between 1495 and 1497, nearly 25% of 1,821 publications by all known presses at the time originated in Venice, while Paris, the second most prolific source, produced about 10% (Lane, 1973, p. 311). As to patents, the city of Florence, Italy, may have issued the first example of a patent in 1421 for the design of a new type of boat.[4]

So, while the concept of intellectual property protection had been long established by the time of the Constitutional Convention in 1787, its importance, thanks to the foresight of the authors, was inserted into the law of the land as Article I, Section 8, Clause 8 of the Constitution of the United States.[5] This clause, the Intellectual Property clause, reads as follows:

> That Congress shall have Power . . . . To promote the Progress of Science and useful Arts, by securing for limited Times to Authors and Inventors the exclusive Right to their respective Writings and Discoveries.

The notion of protecting exclusive rights to "writing and discoveries" means that you actually *own* your written works and inventions as your exclusive property. These products of your mind – your intellect – provided they are original and appear in a tangible form are your property. This is why such things are called "intellectual property" (IP), a somewhat unpleasant legal term of art to apply equally to something as tender and personal as, say, a love poem, as to a mechanical device such as a telephone or elevator or firearm. Venice, the colonies, and the states had all offered intellectual property protections in the past, but the Intellectual Property clause in our constitution, providing a centralized and integrated system for protecting individual creations uniformly across all states, was a unique gift by the constitutional authors to all in the United States.

But, wait. Your ownership is secured for a limited time only. What kind of gift is that? While you can always rightly claim that you first wrote or invented something, you can't keep others from adapting or building on it forever. The reason for this time limit should become clear in a moment. By protecting your intellectual property so only you can commercialize it and get a financial reward, the founders wanted to give you an *incentive* to be creative. They hoped to spur advances in science and useful arts because they knew that such innovations could build the strength of the nation. In this sense, the incentive to create was a personal gift, while the resulting creations can be seen as a gift to the nation. This is why *all* citizens, including those in prison, are potential "authors and inventors" and should be encouraged to "promote the progress of science and useful arts" to benefit the nation regardless of their current address.

Shifting our attention for a moment from the United States to humanity as a whole, we note that the protection of intellectual property can be crucial to improving the lives of people everywhere, a proposition fundamental to the World Intellectual Property Organization (WIPO).[6] Those concerned with global human development have written that IP ultimately helps enhance human capabilities (Fukuda-Parr, 2011, p. xvii). By improving *capabilities*, the author is referring to what economist Amartya Sen argues is the essential ingredient of freedom: "the expansion of the 'capabilities' of persons to lead the kind of lives they value – and have reason to value" (Sen, 1999, p. 18).

Think for a moment about how many innovations in your life allow you to live what you feel is a more valuable life, including innovations that sustain the livelihood you choose to pursue, help you write, communicate, and get around town, and support your fundamental rights, such medical care, food security, speech and access to information, education, cultural expression through a variety of expressive formats, protection from harm, and improved living conditions, to name a few. Intellectual property can improve human capabilities in ways that advance individual freedom in society. But without protecting your right of ownership, at least for a while, you might not be motivated to be creative to begin with. While individual states were well underway creating their own systems for copyright and patent registration by 1787, the constitutional authors wanted federal control of this process, centralized in Congress and unified for all states. This is so that the benefits would be shared nationally, and not just within separate states, which would require inventors and writers to register their claims separately in each and every state, thus creating a disincentive to register or even create to begin with.

In other words, what is established as a constitutional right of individuals (and extended as well to corporate entities), is justified for its value to the entire nation. This is further reinforced by the limitation on the time you have to exploit the commercial value of your creations. For after a certain number of years (which varies between copyrights, trademarks, and patents), your creation can add further benefit to society by eventually becoming available for free use and modification by others.

So far, we have covered the concept of intellectual property and its protection and why the authors of the Constitution wanted to encourage as many people as possible to be creative for socially useful purposes. Why, you might ask, would the constitutional authors be OK with limiting the protection of such intellectual property rights? Indeed, this was a problem back in the day. For the institution of slavery – which built such great wealth among the white population through free Black labor, not only in the South but also at institutions of such renown in the North as Harvard and Yale Universities – stripped ownership of everything from the millions of Black people who were held in bondage (Harvard & the Legacy of Slavery Initiative, 2023, November 13).

Recall that in order to ratify the Constitution, the southern states insisted on preserving their institution of slavery. It took fighting and winning the Civil War to *begin* to rectify this wrong. The process of amending the Constitution to correct this defect has been called by Columbia University historian Eric Foner "The Second Founding" of the nation (Foner, 2019). But, as we will see below, slavery, conditionally defined, remains constitutionally sanctioned, well over 150 years after the end of the Civil War.

Consider for a moment the amount of wealth of authorship and invention that might have been lost to the nation during the time of slavery. This is only hinted at by the emergence of the narratives of escaped slaves at the time. Such stories merited a chapter in cultural historian H. Bruce Franklin's review of prison literature in America, in which he states that American slave narratives contributed a new genre to world literature (Franklin, 1978/1989, p. 5). Consider also the reprisal of old songs formerly sung by enslaved people, later sung by African American convicts picking cotton on a plantation run by a Texas prison in the 20th century (Franklin, 1998). In 1790, some 18% of the total population of the new nation was in human bondage. That is nearly one out of five people! One has only to reflect on the vast treasure of innovations – in music, song, dance, culinary arts, oratory, literature, dress, photography and film, classical and folk art, architecture, and a broad variety of mechanical, cosmetic, and other inventions – given to the nation and indeed the world by Black citizens of the United States *after* the abolishment of slavery in order to appreciate that the opportunity cost caused by suppression of the human creative impulse can indeed impoverish an entire society.

But limiting the protection of intellectual property rights for certain classes of people remains a serious problem for our society today. I am, of course, referring to the people who are now serving time in prison.[7] To get a sense of the size of this population, I have already described it as *Prisonopolis*. But put another way, the prison population in the United States would constitute the 96th largest country on earth, out of 238 countries. That means our prison population is larger than the populations of nearly 40% of the world's nations.

Yet, some may question the direct relationship between the sheer size of a population and the number of copyrights registered or other measures of creativity. The relationship between the size of the population and the discovery of new ideas, or innovation in general, is at the core of many economic growth models, and some fear that a declining population will result in the loss of badly needed innovation overall (Jones, 2022). Yet there are studies skeptical of whether copyright law itself provides an incentive to promote creativity (Ku et al., 2009; Sprigman, 2017). Such circumspection, however, appears to neglect the lack of awareness of copyright protection in the general population. Humans have a creative capacity regardless of intellectual property law, but awareness of IP protection is required to have an effect. It's fair to ask if copyright law should be part of a strategic national effort to proactively encourage creativity among the population. Moreover, a registered copyright can also be a disincentive for a third party to misappropriate the protected work. By encouraging the prison population and indeed the entire population to be creative, by educating them about copyright protection, providing such protection, and giving them the means to share and even sell their works, they will no longer be excluded, or written off by society for their creative potential, as is now largely the case.

I hope you are heartened by this story of how the founders of the nation bequeathed us the salutary gift of IP protection in the Constitution and can see that work remains to extend its blessings to all in the country, including people in prison. Next, I will recount how the modern institution of prison is uniquely, if not intentionally, designed to facilitate the creation of works protected by the Intellectual Property clause of the Constitution of the United States.

Notes

1 See: www.wipo.int/portal/en/, cited 2 May 2024.

2 Note, however, that the current procedures for registering copyright, including the online registration system, are challenging to people in federal prison because the Federal Bureau of Prisons does not allow access to the internet (Federal Bureau of Prisons, 2019, p. 34) and communication by mail is unreliable, given that residency can be changed at any time. Contact the Institute for Intellectual Property and Social Justice for a protocol on how to register a copyright from prison (https://iipsj.org/).

3 Copyright Law Revision, Committee on the Judiciary, Eighty-ninth Congress, First session pursuant to S. Res. 48 on S. 1006 Sess. 65, 1965. See also Lateef Mtima, "Copyright and the Interdependent Relationship Between Social Utility and Social Justice," (Mtima, 2024).
4 Source: www.britannica.com/topic/patent, cited 2 May 2024.
5 Actually, the Committee of Style at the Constitutional Convention was responsible for moving Article VII, Section 1 of the draft of the U.S. Constitution to Article I, Section 8, clearly raising the importance of its provisions (Schwartz, 2022, p. 915)
6 See: www.wipo.int/portal/en/index.html, cited 12 July 2024.
7 People in prison retain their intellectual property rights; however, they are impeded in registering them for protective and other purposes.

References

Federal Bureau of Prisons. (2019). *Legal resource guide to the Federal Bureau of Prisons 2019*. U.S. Department of Justice, Federal Bureau of Prisons. www.bop.gov/resources/pdfs/legal_guide_march_2019.pdf cited 27 September 2023.

Foner, E. (2019). *The second founding: How the Civil War and Reconstruction remade the Constitution*. W.W. Norton & Company.

Franklin, H. B. (1978/1989). *Prison literature in America: The victim as criminal and artist, expanded edition*. Oxford University Press.

Franklin, H. B. (Ed.). (1998). *Prison writing in 20th century America*. Penguin Books.

Fukuda-Parr, S. (2011). Foreword. In T. Wong & G. Dutfield (Eds.), *Intellectual property and human development: Current trends and future scenarios* (pp. xvii–xix). Cambridge University Press.

Hannah-Jones, N., Roper, C., Silverman, I., & Silverstein, J. (Eds.). (2021). *The 1619 project: A new origin story*. One World.

Harvard & the Legacy of Slavery Initiative. (2023, November 13). *Harvard & the legacy of slavery: Reparative partnership grant program, 2023 request for proposals*. www.harvard.edu/vice-provost-for-special-projects/rfp-page/ cited 19 January 2024.

Jones, C. I. (2022). The end of economic growth? Unintended consequences of a declining population. *American Economic Review, 112*(11), 3489–3527.

Ku, R. S. R., Sun, J., & Fan, Y. (2009). Does copyright law promote creativity? An empirical analysis of copyright's bounty. Case Research Paper Series in Legal Studies, Working paper 09-20, 38.

Lane, F. C. (1973). *Venice: A maritime republic*. Johns Hopkins University Press.

Mtima, L. (Ed.). (2015). *Intellectual property, entrepreneurship and social justice: From swords to ploughshares*. Edward Elgar Publishing, Inc.

Mtima, L. (2024). Copyright and the interdependent relationship between social utility and social justice. In S. D. Jamar & L. Mtima (Eds.), *The Cambridge handbook of intellectual property and social justice* (pp. 115–130). Cambridge University Press.

Schwartz, D. S. (2022). Recovering the lost general welfare clause. *William & Mary Law Review*, *63*(3). https://scholarship.law.wm.edu/wmlr/vol63/iss3/4 cited 18 March 2023.

Sen, A. (1999). *Development as freedom*. Knopf.

Sprigman, C. J. (2017). Copyright and creative incentives: What we know (and don't). *Houston Law Review*, *55*(2), 451–478.

Stoner, R., & Dutra, J. (2022). *Copyright industries in the U.S. economy: The 2022 report*. International Intellectual Property Alliance. www.iipa.org/files/uploads/2022/12/IIPA-Report-2022_Interactive_12-12-2022-1.pdf cited 12 July 2024.

Toole, A. A., Miller, R. D., & Rada, N. (2022). *Intellectual property and the U.S. economy* (3rd ed.). United States Patent and Trademark Office. www.uspto.gov/sites/default/files/documents/uspto-ip-us-economy-third-edition.pdf cited 12 July 2024.

Waldstreicher, D. (2019). *Slavery's constitution: From revolution to ratification*. Hill and Wang.

3 How Prison Unintentionally Stokes Creativity

Ironically, prisons evolved throughout history to become – as a totally unintended consequence – a place where creativity could actually have an advantage as compared to the outside world. Perversely, incarceration could potentially be *beneficial* to creativity.[1] The reason, dryly understated by prison writer Saint James Harris Wood, is that the judge gives the incarcerated "some time to write" (Wood, 2022, p. 175).

This is certainly not to say that prisons are a good thing, much less to advocate for prisons as a destination for creative people. But prisons can, in fact, be viewed as a place where people convicted for being a threat to society can and should be encouraged to tap into their talents to make a positive contribution to society for the duration of their sentence, an outcome that should in principle be widely supported. To understand this insight, it is important to consider just how punishment and the role of prisons changed throughout history so that it would come to pass that prisons evolved into a potential wellspring of creativity. Here I provide a brief overview of the origins of involuntary detention and how its function and form evolved over millennia to the institution we know as prison today.

If there is a common theme to variations in punishment and the use of incarceration throughout history, it might be that society adopts ways to punish people that are influenced by population size and other demographics, the type of economy, and prevailing social values. All such features have varied over time and place to influence the form and function of prisons.

Once tribes stopped moving around in search of food and settled down with the advent of agriculture, those in charge of communities growing in population size had to set rules for acceptable behavior and to punish those who misbehaved. Societies tend to thrive when things are stable and dependable so people can attend to their affairs in security without disruption. Social values of agrarian and community tranquility and security replaced those among bands of hunters valuing mobility and surprise assaults. Records unearthed through archaeology provide evidence that rulers started laying down laws to govern social behavior in the earliest known human settlements,

DOI: 10.4324/9781003566021-4

stressing the importance of protection and security in the new demography of concentrated living.

The first known references to a legally designated place of detention in Western civilization appear about 4,000 years ago in a set of codes or laws written in Sumer and Babylon in the region of Mesopotamia situated in modern Iraq (ca. 2100 BCE), as well as in the Law of Moses, or Mosaic Law (ca. 1500 BCE), which emerged in the area of Mount Sinai shortly after the Mesopotamian codes.[2] These Mesopotamian and Mosaic edicts were similar in that they were both divinely inspired and enumerated sets of behavioral conditions written in the structural form: "If you do this [crime], then you will suffer this [punishment]." Many codes specified the consequences of economic crimes and made reference to slaves. Although polytheistic (Hammurabi received the codes directly from Shamash, the Sun-god), the Mesopotamians established codes that were generally *secular* in nature, implying that transgressions were considered a threat to society. In contrast, the monotheistic Hebrews wrote laws that were *religious* in nature and invoked the concept of transgressions against their god, reflecting a key difference in social values between the Mesopotamian and Mosaic societies (Davies, 1905, pp. 8, 12).[3]

The divine origin of such codes, whether Mesopotamian or Mosaic, provides a socially acceptable legitimacy for using such laws as the basis to judge and punish people. Humanly fabricated laws might be seen as arbitrary or motivated by self-interest, but laws delivered from the gods, or in the case of the Israelites, by *their one* god, would ensure unquestionable social acceptance. Both types of regulations, Mesopotamian and Mosaic, included retribution by retaliation in kind, "An eye for an eye, a tooth for a tooth," known in law as *lex talionis* (related to the word "retaliation"). Compare, for example, the following Hammurabi and Mosaic versions (Davies, 1905, p. 85):

> Hammurabi Code: 196. If a man destroy the eye of another man, one shall destroy his eye.
> Mosaic Code: Thou shalt give life for life, eye for eye, tooth for tooth, hand for hand, foot for foot, burning for burning, wound for wound, strike for strike.
>
> (Ex. 21:24, 25. See also Lev. 24:20; Deut. 19:21)

These codes made occasional references to an administrative place of short-term detention to hold an individual until punished, which might involve payment of a fine, some form of bodily dismemberment or disfigurement, such as cutting off the hand of a thief (corporal punishment), or death (capital punishment). Examples from early Mesopotamian sources have also been found that indicate detention in prison as a form of punitive retribution for as long as 45 months, not merely as a temporary holding pen while awaiting corporal or financial penalty, as well as imprisonment as a means to reform, not only to punish, the transgressor (Reid, 2016).

Ancient Greece presents a fascinating case because here we have the first notions, in Western history, of democracy as a form of social arrangement combined with deep philosophical deliberation concerning the psychology of crime and the institutional nature of punishment and how it fits awkwardly in the ideal concept of democracy. The bricks-and-mortar Athenian jail is not itself the subject of intrigue, for it simply served that era's purpose as a temporary holding pen. The innovation of interest appears in Plato's various dialogues, particularly the *Laws*, in which characters discuss prison and punishment. As philosophy scholar Jacob Abolafia describes (Abolafia, 2021), Plato's conception of the prison can be seen as anticipating the modern penal institution where transgressors serve for extended periods in order to undergo education to correct their misguided understanding or ignorance of what is right; in other words, what today we might call correction or rehabilitation. The disconnection between such criminal reform and democracy lies in Plato's conception that the diagnosis and treatment of transgressors is beyond the capacity of democratically selected citizen juries and requires instead an elite corps of those who have knowledge of what is right. Given this allusion to the ancient Greeks, Abolafia suggests that the conception of a reformatory prison may not have originated so recently, as Michel Foucault and other scholars suggest (Abolafia, 2021, p. 83).

In the period of Roman civilization in Europe, ranging from about 600 BCE to about 500 CE, we see some innovative forms of detention and punishment emerge. According to the historian of ancient Rome Mary Beard, Julius Caesar may have offered the first instance of prison as a place for life-long detention as punishment for a group of rebels who tried to topple the Roman government in 63 BCE. She notes that this would have been the "first time in Western history" to propose life imprisonment (Beard, 2015, pp. 34–35). Maybe, but the seditionists were executed anyway. Perhaps the most entertaining, but no less gruesome, punitive innovation was the use of criminals, slaves, and prisoners of war as gladiators fighting animals and each other to the death in colosseums for the amusement of the public and, of course, their rulers. The famous Colosseum of Rome was completed in 80 CE.

Eventually, the Catholic Church and its Christian doctrine of monotheism, selected by Roman Emperor Constantine in 330 CE to replace the popular practice of polytheism, assumed the leading role in regulating social arrangements in Europe. As with Mosaic Law among the ancient Hebrews, its religious precepts became the basis for passing judgment on social behavior with severe consequences for transgressions against Church beliefs. Notable punishments included confinement in monasteries and burning at the stake. Showing softer, perhaps New Testament values, Constantine himself replaced death by crucifixion with hanging and ordered that slaves be branded on their feet rather than on their faces. I'll call that reform. Places of detention typically were still temporary stops on the way to terminal punishment.

In the Middle Ages of Europe, ranging from about 500 to 1500 CE, following the collapse of the Roman Empire, which created the threat of a Hobbesian vacuum of protective state control, we see a form of social order emerge organized as networks of mutual protection established between more powerful, land-owning men and their weaker dependents. Feudal chiefs maintained order among vassals and serfs living in the lord's manor and on his land (Bloch, 1961/1964). In conditions of general judicial flux and disorder during this period, chiefs assumed judicial control over their subjects, though there were also territorial courts of high justice. Only the most odious of crimes resulted in capital punishment. Fines were more common, and references to prisoners seem to be reserved for enemies taken in combat.

As people increasingly moved to and concentrated in cities, creating a new urban demographic, new political forms of organization emerged along with novel forms of torturous punishment. French sociologist Michel Foucault, opens his book, *Discipline & Punishment: The Birth of the Prison*, with a horrifying account of retribution imposed on a prisoner named Robert-François Damiens, delivered through a barbaric, publicly displayed suite of corporal and capital punishments in mid-18th-century France (Foucault, 1977, p. 3). The denouement of Damiens' execution for attempting (without success) to kill King Louis XV requires two and a half more pages of vivid description in Foucault's book and was even more terrifying and ghastly than his grim opening paragraph would suggest.[4]

As Foucault explains, the focus on the body as the object of punishment gave way to a new form of punishment, one focused on the soul. The practice of capital punishment ceased to be a public spectacle and began to be conducted in relative privacy, with a physician looking on, and the apparatus of death also transformed from the scaffold and the guillotine to the administration of drugs, commencing with a pain reliever to make the experience of death less traumatic. Again, we see a change in social values reflected in the nation's practice of punishment.

This shift from the body to the soul as the target of retribution introduced new complications. It meant that decisions had to be made on the miscreant's term of detention. And the soul as the object of retribution demanded consideration of the mental state of the defendant and the possibility of insanity as a criminal defense. Foucault notes that despite the shift to the soul as the object of retribution, the body itself nevertheless continued to suffer assault through hunger, punishment, solitary confinement, and sexual deprivation (Foucault, 1977, pp. 15–16).

This transitional period of punitive "reforms" lasted a mere century, from about the early- to mid-1700s to the mid-1800s, though the exact timing of change varied across countries. The shift from public spectacles of bodily torture to more prosaic and less visible quotidian acts of vengeance suffered at the hands of guards in deplorable conditions of confinement during long-term imprisonment is essentially a substitution of one sadistic form of retributive depravity for another. Reforms may have improved matters for the authorities, but not necessarily for the people at their mercy.

Before the American Revolution, colonial authorities promulgated the same tortuous penalties reminiscent of Damien's execution in the same era but applied to people held in bondage. As Bryan Stevenson recounts in *The 1619 Project*, enslavement entailed brutality, including bodily dismemberment, decapitation, and quartering for public display (Stevenson, 2021, p. 278). In 1682, William Penn, a leading Quaker and founder of what would become Pennsylvania, having himself experienced imprisonment in England's Newgate Prison, passed a law allowing a period of confinement as an alternative to capital punishment (Rubin, 2019, p. 280).

The American Revolution provided a unique opportunity for the new nation to repudiate England's notorious prisons and start anew toward what would eventually become the contemporary prison. Employing extended detention as an alternative to capital punishment was inspired by prior penal reform doctrines, one by Italian aristocrat Cesare Beccaria, writing in the period 1762 to 1766 (Bellamy, 1995/2003); the other by British sheriff John Howard in 1777. Sociologist and prison scholar Ashley T. Rubin describes how the contemporary innovation of prison as a facility for long-term punitive incarceration, as distinct from jails used for temporary holding purposes, emerged first as state-run prisons in the post-Revolutionary United States. Such prisons emerged in Massachusetts at the Castle Island military fort in Boston harbor in 1785; atop a copper mine in Connecticut called New-Gate in 1790; and at the Walnut Street Jail in Philadelphia, Pennsylvania, in 1794 (Rubin, 2019). All required hard labor during extended sentences, but Walnut Street also featured a number of reforms, including the separation of types of offenders and segregation by sex; cleanliness; health; good maintenance of the facility; a salaried jailer to address corruption; and, though affecting relatively few residents, solitary confinement. These three models, or "proto-prisons," provided what Rubin terms "templates" that could be replicated by other states, the first of a series of competing templates to emerge during the process of penal organization and practice in the United States (Rubin, 2019).

As Rubin describes, these proto-prison models failed to meet expectations, with Walnut Street experiencing overcrowding and sickness, prompting New York and Pennsylvania to design new carceral templates, larger facilities designed to overcome overcrowding and looming facades to evoke fear. Eventually, the *Pennsylvania System*, featuring solitary confinement for all residents in their cells, where they would undertake menial labor such as weaving and shoe-making, competed against New York's *Auburn System* (a.k.a. the Congregate or Silent System), in which residents spent their nights in solitary cells but joined with others during the day in factory-type labor but forbidden to talk or even look at each other.

The Auburn System prevailed as a standard during the period between 1820 and 1860. Also during this period, word of prison reforms in America reached Europe, motivating some Europeans to inspect these innovations in the newborn nation for themselves. Gustave de Beaumont and Alexis de Tocqueville, young French aristocrats, were commissioned by their government to travel to America in 1831 and report back on its penitentiary system. Following their return to France, they argued in favor of adopting America's reforms. Beaumont wrote most of the report for the government (Beaumont & Tocqueville, 1833/1964). Tocqueville wrote his own book, *Democracy in America*, which includes the following, terse reference to his penal fact-finding trip: "For the first time the idea of reforming offenders as well as punishing them penetrated into the prisons" (Tocqueville, 1835/1969, p. 250).[5] The innovation of reforming "offenders" was noteworthy in a report on the new democracy.

Charles Dickens, across the Channel from France, whose father had spent time in Marshalsea debtors prison in London, conducted his own survey of American prisons, traveling from England to America in 1842. He wrote of deplorable conditions in the Philadelphia Eastern Penitentiary, "a plan peculiar to the state of Pennsylvania. The system here, is rigid, strict, and hopeless solitary confinement. I believe it, in its effects, to be cruel and wrong." (Dickens, 1913, p. 81). Among the residents Dickens observed were spent souls, some sick, and even a young, "coloured boy" imprisoned with adults, while white children were safely isolated elsewhere among themselves, inspiring Dickens to remark about class privilege (p. 81).

By the Civil War, the Auburn System template had become the preferred model for replication in all states with the exception, of course, of Pennsylvania. The Civil War caused somewhat of a tectonic upheaval, in that the armies of the North destroyed Southern prisons, and eventual emancipation cratered the supply of free labor in its economy. The South then embarked on a project to re-engineer slavery. Southern states created new laws based on fabricating a web of minor transgressions, such as vagrancy, designed to entrap and imprison Black people. These laws were known as the Black Codes. Duly convicted of crimes, Blacks could be put to work in "involuntary servitude," a.k.a. "slavery," thanks to the postbellum 13th Constitutional Amendment of 1865. Southern ingenuity then devised a variety of new carceral templates: *convict leasing* stationed the convicted in business enterprises needing cheap labor; *chain gangs* organized the convicted, chained together, to build public infrastructure, including the streets of Atlanta; and *prison farms*, or penal farms, which housed the convicted on plantations to labor in the cotton and tobacco fields exactly as their enslaved predecessors, sometimes under the watchful gaze of an armed, white prisoner. Alas, although chained, they eased their toil by chanting stories together, signaling the emergence of a new form of expressive creativity in carceral context beyond previous, isolated examples of graffiti or rough art drawn or carved on prison walls. Musicologist Alan Lomax recorded a number of their singsong field chants from 1943 through the end of the Jim Crow era (Campbell et al., 2016).

While various template innovations, such as they were, replaced the Auburn-style prisons in the South, it is important to note that extralegal forms of post-Revolutionary punishment were also enthusiastically pursued, largely, but not exclusively in the South. Barbaric vigilantism, practiced with the tacit consent of the law, terrorized Blacks with impunity from Reconstruction to World War II. Social justice activist Bryan Stevenson reminds us of over 4,400 lynchings during this era, some involving mobs dismembering fingers, impaling their victims with corkscrews, and burning them alive before crowds of whites feasting on "deviled eggs and lemonade" (2021, pp. 280–281).

As the South was regressing in the postbellum period, northern prisons were experiencing overcrowding, which led to creating separate facilities for women and also for youth and first-time offenders who were deemed suitable for reform, and thus *reformatories* were born. Hard-core offenders were separately accommodated in re-designed Auburn-like prisons, now called *maximum-security prisons*.

Before 1891, federal prisoners were detained in state facilities. That year, Congress passed the Three Prisons Act, establishing a Federal Prison System, launching federal operation of three prisons – Leavenworth, McNeil Island, and Atlanta. The Federal Prison System was succeeded in 1930 with the inauguration of the Federal Bureau of Prisons (BOP) to oversee the nation's 11 federal prisons housing 14,115 residents at the time.[6]

Rubin (2019) describes the further evolution of prison templates in the 1920s and 30s, with the construction of *Big House prisons*, larger than previous buildings to accommodate thousands of new residents. Then, following World War II, yet a new template emerged, the *correctional institution*, along with collateral neologisms such as "inmate," "correctional officer," and "treatment staff" (p. 289). With California's facilities leading the way, education, vocational training, therapy, even in a specialized format called bibliotherapy, would be applied to rehabilitate, or correct, the convicted, evocative of Plato's ancient carceral ideal. This could not have happened without the confluence of social values favoring rehabilitation and the duration of incarceration extended long enough to provide time for such enlightenment. Momentously, in the millennial-long gestation of penal reform arrives the *birth of sanctioned creative potential in prison*. Prison could now embody the nexus of confinement and creation, stoking education, learning, and creativity among residents poised to flourish from their time in detention. As we will see in the next chapter, this moment brought forth a raft of new arts-in-corrections and other educational initiatives that were transformative in their effect on residents. It took 2,000 years, but Plato would have been delighted.

Then, in the 1980s and 1990s, the nation's social values took a conservative turn and its carceral attitude darkened again. Rehabilitation programs, including Pell Grants for the incarcerated, were terminated and tough-on-crime bills, enforced with bellicose fervor, virtually harvested young men, mostly Black, off the streets and locked them up. To accommodate the prison population explosion, the nation launched an unprecedented and politically popular construction campaign to build so-called *warehouse prisons*. This trend, in turn, spawned yet another novel prison template tailored for the most hardened of offenders, the *supermaximum-security prison* (supermax) (Rubin, 2019, pp. 288–289). Once again, overcrowding, as well as newly introduced and divisive racial, ethnic, and gang-related factors began to overwhelm the ability of corrections officers to ensure order and safety leading to extreme measures such as lock-downs and long-term solitary confinement, penal practices that continue to characterize the contemporary prison in America.

At last, we can see how this long process of prison evolution reached a stage conducive to carceral creativity. This was first glimpsed in the short-lived period following the birth of the correctional institution, notably in California. Situated in the contemporary prison, the prison resident has all the time in the world to devote to cultivating his or her creative talents. What is needed going forward is a creative carceral policy ensuring supervisory tolerance, indeed promotion, of creative engagement, not only for resident rehabilitation but also for societal benefit. Elements of such a policy can be found in existing sources. We might, for example, consult the Council of Europe Recommendations on Education in Prison, notably recommendation 12, which states, "Creative and cultural activities should be given a significant role because these activities have particular potential to enable prisoners to develop and express themselves."[7] Implicit in this recommendation, as elaborated in this book, is that such activities would also benefit the nation. This is confirmed by a European Union management authority, Corrado Marcetti, writing in a report on prisons in Europe, "inside the prison systems of Europe the production of cultural and artistic events can very often create excellent results and can contribute on a general scale to the development of culture and art in society" (Fondazione Giovanni Michelucci, 2013, p. 11).

The concept of carceral creativity offers an opportunity to reorient the oft-repeated purpose of prison from retribution, incapacitation, deterrence, and rehabilitation to a more modern and humanitarian one of restoration – restoring the human capacity for reflection and constructive social engagement; regeneration – revitalizing the initial promise and energy to become a productive citizen; and redemption – rectifying an erroneous judgment about one's intrinsic value to society as the basis for a new vision and start in life. All of these goals can be advanced through engagement in the creative arts. California's erstwhile leadership in creative carceral policy showed us what is possible through a renewed, nationwide commitment to put the dimension of time in penal sentencing to its best use within the carceral facility, for its administration, its residents, and society.

Notes

1 This insight was suggested to me by IP law scholar Lateef Mtima.
2 I focus on Western civilization in this book; however, prison appears in historical records in China some 4,000 years ago, as well, between 2205 BCE and 2198 BCE (Zhou, 1991).
3 William Walter Davies (1848–1922) was a professor of modern languages and Hebrew at Ohio Wesleyan University (https://ohio5.contentdm.oclc.org/digital/collection/p15963coll29/id/7566/, cited 18 July 2024).
4 Foucault's opening is sensational, but this repertoire of serial inflictions was not common. It was previously wreaked on the regicide François Revaillac in 1610 and never repeated after Damiens' botched ordeal (Spierenburg, 1995/1998, p. 44). Many varieties of corporeal and capital punishment were more common: mutilation, breaking (bones) on the wheel, execution by decapitation (honorable) or hanging (nonhonorable), whipping, branding, garroting, burial alive, and strangling, to name a few (Spierenburg, 1995/1998).
5 Beaumont would also write his own book, *Marie*, a novel about slavery in America (Beaumont, 1958).
6 See a Bureau of Prisons timeline here: www.bop.gov/about/history/timeline.jsp, and a history of corrections here: https://nicic.gov/resources/nic-library/hot-topics/history-corrections-america, cited 27 September 2023.
7 See: www.epea.org/council-of-europe-recommendations-on-education-in-prison/, cited 15 May 2024.

References

Abolafia, J. (2021). Plato's theory of incarceration. *Ramus*, *50*(1&2), 68–86.
Beard, M. (2015). *SPQR: A history of ancient Rome*. Liveright Publishing Corporation.
Beaumont, G. D. (1958). *Marie, or, slavery in the United States*. The Johns Hopkins University Press.
Beaumont, G. D., & Tocqueville, A. D. (1833/1964). *On the penitentiary system in the United states and its application in France* (F. Lieber, Trans.). Southern Illinois University Press.
Bellamy, R. (Ed.). (1995/2003). *Beccaria: On crimes and punishments and other writings*. Cambridge University Press.
Bloch, M. (1961/1964). *Feudal society: Volume 1: The growth of ties of dependence*. The University of Chicago Press.
Campbell, L., Harvey, T., Warman, B., Willer, C., & Wogan, H. (2016). *Alan Lomax discography*. American Folklife Center, Library of Congress. www.loc.gov/static/collections/alan-lomax-manuscripts/documents/Lomax_discography_master.pdf cited 25 February 2024.

Davies, W. W. (1905). *Codes of Hammurabi and Moses*. The Methodist Book Concern.

Dickens, C. (1913). *American notes for general circulation and pictures from Italy*. Chapman and Hall Ltd. www.gutenberg.org/cache/epub/675/pg675-images.html cited 19 July 2023.

Fondazione Giovanni Michelucci (Ed.). (2013). *Art and culture in prison*. www.epea.org/wp-content/uploads/Art-and-Culture-i-Prison-publication.pdf

Foucault, M. (1977). *Discipline & punish: The birth of the prison* (A. Sheridan, Trans.). Vintage Books.

Reid, J. N. (2016). The birth of the prison: The functions of imprisonment in early Mesopotamia. *Journal of Ancient Near Eastern History*, *3*(2), 81–115.

Rubin, A. T. (2019). History of the prison. In M. Deflem (Ed.), *The handbook of social control* (pp. 279–292). John Wiley and Sons. https://doi.org/10.1002/9781119372394.ch20

Spierenburg, P. (1995/1998). The body and the state: Early modern Europe. In N. Morris & D. J. Rothman (Eds.), *The Oxford history of the prison* (pp. 44–70). Oxford University Press.

Stevenson, B. (2021). Punishment. In N. Hannah-Jones, C. Roper, I. Silverman, & J. Silverstein (Eds.), *The 1619 project: A new origin story* (pp. 275–283). One World.

Tocqueville, A. D. (1835/1969). *Democracy in America* (G. Lawrence, Trans.). Harper & Row.

Wood, S. J. H. (2022). On publishing from prison. In C. Meissner (Ed.), *The sentences that create us: Crafting a writer's life in prison* (pp. 175–179). Haymarket Books and PEN America.

Zhou, J. (1991). The Chinese correctional system and its development. *International Journal of Comparative and Applied Criminal Justice*, *15*(1), 15–32.

4 Creators in Print

The case for a national carceral creativity policy has so far explored the premises of a universal human impulse for creativity, an inclusive approach to the constitutionally grounded imperative to promote creativity for the benefit of the nation combined with a recognition of the opportunity cost in failing to be inclusive, and a carceral venue that promises sufficient time for a resident to learn and apply creative skills for beneficial purposes. I now turn to the evidence of various types of creative works that have emerged from prison, affirmation that I hope will convince readers that we should prevent obstructing such creativity, and, moreover, to encourage and support more such engagement. In this chapter, I recount brief examples of creativity in detention from secondary sources. In the next chapter, I will offer short cases of currently incarcerated creators with examples of their work drawn from primary sources, the creators themselves.

There are numerous, published historical and contemporary examples of important works created in prisons. Richard Brower, himself an artist as well as psychologist, explored the historical record of prominent creators who landed in jail, noting the "essential tension between creativity and conformity" (Brower, 1999, p. 3). Brower describes different historical eras characterized as having a Zeitgeist, or cultural temperament, that is either repressive, by strictly imposing conformity, or looser, by allowing greater expressive freedom, and that the prevailing social Zeitgeist can explain the incarceration of artists in various media. But, of course, creators with no prior experience in the arts can be born, as it were, while incarcerated, and the Zeitgeist within the prison walls can similarly repress or encourage creativity.

Here, I organize accounts of notable creativity in only a few expressive categories – literature, visual arts, and music – to establish that the deeply rooted human impulse to create ineluctably takes shape in ways that are manifestly useful to society. You will likely recognize the names of many of these creators.

DOI: 10.4324/9781003566021-5

Literature

Prison writing is a genre of literary works created by incarcerated people during or after their detention. Educator Grady Hillman invokes John Donne, Daniel Defoe, Honoré de Balzac, Fyodor Dostoevsky, Oscar Wilde, William Sydney Porter, alias O. Henry, Etheridge Knight, Michael Hogan, John Minarik, Merle Haggard, Miguel Pinero, Edward Bunker, and Jean Genet among the many examples of creative prison writers (Hillman, 2023, pp. 3, 17). Like the blade of green grass that emerges from the barren cracks of a concrete wasteland, we have seen people in prison held in the most infertile conditions express their creative capacities. The prison experience has also inspired former residents to tell their stories following release. Prison writing is confirmation that creators, while in prison or afterward, share the impulse to convert their creative talents into tangible gifts of value to society.

First I will note prison writers who exemplify a privileged class in their societies. Their "crimes" were due to political activity, economic greed, or engagement in acts deemed immoral at the time, examples of what we might call *socioeconomic-political transgressors*. Then I will present prison writers *born into deprivation* in underserved communities. Their experiences and environments reveal troubling characteristics that are worthy of greater policy attention by those truly interested in preventing or reducing crime by abolishing poverty. Finally, I will address several valuable *collections and anthologies* of prison writing.

Socioeconomic-Political Transgressors

Prison writing offers examples of people who were locked up for offending political powers, committing crimes in protest of government policies, violating business or moral codes, such as committing crimes due to financial addiction or greed or poor judgment, or because of a condition deemed pathological. Julian Broadhead, in *Unlocking the Prison Muse*, deliberately excludes political prisoners from his account of prison writing as a means for personal transformation in Britain (Broadhead, 2006), but here I adopt the more inclusive definition of a "political prisoner" as "applied to anyone confined for a politically motivated offense, violent or nonviolent" (Neier, 1995/1998, p. 351). To be included here, an author must have created works during or after imprisonment.

Boethius (c. 480–524 CE) was a Roman politician imprisoned for treason (actually for calling out government corruption) by his Ostrogothic king, Theoderic the Great. He wrote *The Consolation of Philosophy* on the nature of fortune and misfortune in confinement and was considered the last Christian martyr for his ordeal of torture and execution (Peters, 1995, p. 23).

Florentine Niccolò Machiavelli (1469–1527), popularly known for his timeless advice to rulers on how they should conduct themselves in the best interest of the territories under their control, including cruelty when necessary, found himself facing execution in 1513. According to *Machiavelli in Hell*, a book by political philosopher Sebastian De Grazia, we find the coach sitting in his prison writing sonnets, one of which refers to lice as big as butterflies and a stench redolent of the dead soldiers massacred at Roncesvalles (1994, p. 34). The lice need no explanation. Roncesvalles was a town in northern Spain in which Charlemagne's army was decimated by the Basques, leaving behind masses of rotting corpses, Machiavelli's olfactory allusion. But the actual stench he experienced may have originated from nearby animal decomposition, not from within the prison.

The poet's sonnets further describe conditions inside the prison, including the type of torture he endured there. Yet he earnestly counsels princely leaders to employ cruelty to keep subjects united and loyal (Machiavelli, 1532/2008, p. 57), advice De Grazia explains as a means to inspire fear of the prince (De Grazia, 1994, p. 36).

William Penn (1644–1718), the English writer and devout Quaker who with other Quakers founded the Province of Pennsylvania (now the state), was himself imprisoned for blasphemy several times in the late 1600s. He wrote *No Cross, No Crown*, and *The Great Case for Liberty and Conscience* in the Tower of London and subsequently would argue for a more progressive vision of prison, sentencing residents to workshops and ending the death penalty except for murder and treason (Murphy, 2015, pp. 337, 339; Neier, 1995/1998, p. 352).

The French Marquis de Sade (1740–1814), whose name is associated with sadism, wrote a number of works, including short stories, plays, political essays, and libertine novels featuring vivid descriptions, mostly while imprisoned for numerous engagements in sexual deviance (Perrottet, 2015). He penned *120 Days of Sodom* inside the Bastille just prior to the French Revolution. In Vincennes prison, he was allowed a library of 600 books, armchairs, and a desk for writing. While in Charenton, an insane asylum, he organized theatrical productions to entertain both prison residents and high society patrons.

Italian political dissident Silvio Pellico (1789–1854) wrote a lengthy account titled, *My Prisons*, on doing time from 1820 to 1830, initially at Santa Margherita prison, later at the Piombi prison inside the Doge's palace in Venice, then followed by Spielberg prison at Brno, Czechoslovakia (Pellico, 1836). The book was published in 1836. During his imprisonment – his initial sentence of death was later commuted to 15 years – he authored a number of tragedies. His memoirs of prison, translated at the time throughout Europe, were seen as aiding the unification of Italy following Austrian occupation.

In 1846, Henry David Thoreau (1817–1862) spent only one night in jail in Concord, Massachusetts, for refusing to pay six years of poll taxes. This inspired him to write in *Civil Disobedience* that his imprisonment was a foolish way to neglect the services he might otherwise have to offer to society (1849–1863/1993, p. 284). Thoreau's writing would influence Mahatma Gandhi's commitment to nonviolence, which, in turn, influenced Martin Luther King, Jr.'s.

Fyodor Dostoyevsky (1821–1881) recounted his imprisonment at Omsk for four years starting in 1849 for participating in a group that discussed French socialists in his *Memoirs From the House of the Dead* (Neier, 1995/1998, p. 354).

In 1873, 29-year-old French poet Paul Verlaine (1844–1896) was imprisoned for two years for shooting his kindred spirit and *amoureux*, Arthur Rimbaud, aged 18, nonfatally hitting his wrist (Bernstein, 1965, p. xxvii). He is said to have created sketches and produced some of his finest poetry behind bars (Willsher, 2015, October 17).

In 1897, English author Oscar Wilde (1854–1900) wrote *De Profundis* in prison, a deep reflection on how society abuses people who, regardless of their personal integrity and brilliant contributions to society – in this case, his literary prowess – can be imprisoned for not conforming to majority sexual norms even when of mutual consent. Later, while in exile, Wilde also wrote *Ballad of Reading Gaol* about a hanging that took place during his imprisonment (Carnochan, 1995; Spierenburg, 1995/1998, p. 385).

Bertrand Russell (1872–1970), the famous English mathematician and philosopher, ended up in Brixton Prison in 1919 for protesting United States engagement on behalf of England in World War I. In his autobiography, Russell wrote how his incarceration was "agreeable," with no interruptions and the opportunity to write *Introduction to Mathematical Philosophy* and to begin writing *Analysis of the Mind* (Neier, 1995/1998, pp. 357–358).

Fascism as a political ideology opposed to communism was born in Italy with the rise of Benito Mussolini (Paxton, 2004, p. 5), and by 1928, Mussolini's government had caught up with Italian communist organizer Antonio Gramsci (1891–1937) and imprisoned him until shortly before his death. While in prison, he authored some 2,848 pages of notebooks about many aspects of political philosophy. His work was published posthumously in *Selections from the Prison Notebooks* (Gramsci, 1971/2003). One of Gramsci's enduring insights was to refine the concept he called "social hegemony" to explain how a dominant group in a nation is able to achieve acceptance of its preferences by the general population even when such preferences are harmful to the population. One method of enforcing the dominant group's preferences is to "legally" impose discipline on those who do not "consent" (Gramsci, 1971/2003, p. 12).

American poet Ezra Pound (1885–1972), who influenced writers including Ernest Hemingway and James Joyce, also had stubborn streaks of anti-Semitism, pro-fascism, and anti-capitalism. Between 1941 and 1945, Pound, living in Italy, was paid by the Italians to deliver propaganda by radio, praising Mussolini and Hitler and calling for American soldiers to lay down their arms. He was subsequently held for treason by the U.S. military and placed in a steel cage near Pisa, Italy in 1945. While in custody, Pound began writing what became *The Pisan Cantos*, his longest work, a portion of which was drafted on toilet paper.

In the United States, some 125,000 ethnic Japanese, most born in America, were sent to internment camps during World War II years 1942 to 1946,[1] in which many residents resorted to creating visual arts and artifacts. The Japanese word to describe this practice is "gaman," which means "to bear the seemingly unbearable with patience and dignity."[2] Residents also created literature in various forms in either English or Japanese, including *Treadmill*, a novel reportedly written while in detention by Hiroshi Nakamura (1996).[3] Nakamura uses the device of the novel to convey the experience of racism against ethnic Japanese as well as the psychology of mobilizing citizens against an enemy, pitting citizen against citizen within a country as well as against those in another, noting that "people must be taught to hate and fear before they can be persuaded to kill" (Nakamura, 1996, p. 23).

Alexander Solzhenitsyn (1918–2008) was sentenced in 1945 to eight years in a labor camp for anti-Soviet propaganda followed by internal exile, providing him with material for several books including *The Gulag Archipelago* about Soviet labor camps, to which Stalin had sent some estimated seven million to 12 million people (Neier, 1995/1998, p. 362).

Nelson Mandela (1918–2013) was sent to Pretoria Local Prison in South Africa after his trial in 1962 and subsequently moved to Robben Island Prison, then Pollsmoor Prison, and lastly Victor Verster Prison before his release in 1990. While in prison, he wrote letters, 255 of which have been assembled in *The Prison Letters of Nelson Mandela*, published in 2018.

One of the most celebrated and fitting examples evoking Shelley's "Prometheus Unbound" is a jailed Martin Luther King, Jr. (1929–1968), suffering woes and defying power to hope to achieve good, great, joyous, beautiful, freedom for Black people. His testament, "Letter from Birmingham City Jail," written in 1963, is not only a supreme example of literature but also a moral statement that continues to provide hugely consequential value for the rest of society and the world. One passage states that freedom must be demanded by the oppressed (p. 91). This evokes the often-quoted dictum of Frederick Douglass, that "Power concedes nothing without a demand. It never did and it never will . . .. The limits of tyrants are prescribed by the endurance of those whom they oppress" (Douglass, 1857).

Jesuit priest, anti-war activist, and poet Daniel Berrigan (1921–2016) served three years in a federal prison in Danbury, Connecticut, for destroying government records in 1968 and then evading the FBI until 1970. His poems included in *The Light from Another Country: Poetry from American Prisons* evoke his prison experience (Bruchac, 1984, pp. 43–47).

Human rights activist Aryeh Neier's chapter, "Confining Dissent" in the *Oxford History of the Prison* (Neier, 1995/1998) provides numerous examples of political prisoners. Some of these have written about their experiences, including Chinese political prisoners Liu Binyan, *A Higher Kind of Loyalty* (1990), Nien Cheng, *Life and Death in Shanghai* (1987), Argentine editor and publisher Jacobo Timerman, *Prisoner without a Name, Cell without a Number* (1981), and Polish political writer Adam Michnik, whose writings from prison helped to end Communist rule in his country (1983). He closes his chapter by writing that imprisoned dissenters represent a disproportionate number of exceptional thinkers and writers of the time (p. 379).

Inspired by recently released anarchist Eric King, prison abolitionist Josh Davidson collected some 30 accounts from other such political activists, currently or recently incarcerated, in *Rattling the Cages: Oral Histories of North American Political Prisoners* (Davidson & King, 2023). Each account addresses sections on prison life, politics and prison dynamics, and the future. At nearly 400 pages, this collection is a contemporary account of the political prisoner's experience and a reminder of the many ways one can so easily become entangled in the carceral web for engaging in principled resistance.

Corruption in a business context is typically considered a white-collar crime. The individuals involved likely did not engage in illegal activities due to deprivation or material hardship, but more out of financial greed or simply by miscalculating risk. Thus, in 1998, Piper Kerman went to federal prison for 13 months for money laundering for a drug enterprise. Her memoir, *Orange Is the New Black*, first published in 2010, documents her experience in prison (Kerman, 2011).

Born Into Deprivation

Certain social determinants of prison appear to be especially acute in underserved and segregated communities. In contrast to the authors listed earlier, those below entered the world in conditions of severe privation characterized by racial segregation, economic poverty, poor housing, poor education, few jobs, no living wage, crime, violence, sex crimes, drugs, alcohol, and gangs. The influence of parental behavior and community social norms, particularly peer pressure, can influence a young mind in ways that lead to poor choices. Specific categories of trauma are shown to have a relationship to later, adult mortality (Felitti et al., 1998). Ten such categories, used to determine the Adverse Childhood Experiences (ACE) score,[4] include witnessing domestic violence, childhood neglect, and having a household member go to prison. Exposure has been shown not only to lead to poor adult health and behavioral conditions but also to increase the risk of engagement in the juvenile justice system (Graf et al., 2021) and to influence the development of white supremacists (Windisch et al., 2022).

In the United Kingdom, Sally-Ann Ashton, a scientist studying juvenile crime, provides an analysis of how adolescent white males become engaged in violent offending (Ashton, 2023). She finds that community-based characteristics, peer pressures, and family dynamics can overcome in a youth's mind what we might assume to be more rational choices. And severe poverty as well as the absence of legitimate opportunities for income make crime the only apparent option. Even childhood exposure to traffic-related air pollution and lead in the neighborhood has been shown to lower income in adulthood compared to their parents and to increase the probability of incarceration and teen motherhood for both Black and white children (Manduca & Sampson, 2021).

Concentrated areas in which deprivation is common include communities of color, and given the particular history of the racist treatment of Blacks in the United States, this should be no surprise. The notion that prison should serve as a deterrent to any rational person in such communities characterized by norms of violence largely imposed by racial divisiveness is misguided. The rational calculus of a youth living in such a community is one of survival and meeting basic human needs. Jack Henry Abbott, a white prison writer known for his book, *In the Belly of the Beast*, who took the lives of others and so might be assumed to lack empathy, issued a stark indictment of white people when he wrote that Black people were treated so poorly by whites that violence and hatred by Blacks is, in his mind, justified (Abbott, 1981, p. 148). Abbott himself had a troubled origin story, recounted below. But here, Abbott refers to the maltreatment of Blacks resulting in the loss of their sense of self-worth. As James Baldwin explains in *The Fire Next Time*, such victims "would do anything whatever to regain it. This is why the most dangerous creation of any society is that man who has nothing to lose" (Baldwin, 1962/1998, p. 330).

Some of the voices below were starting to show signs of extraordinary promise before being overtaken by bad luck, poor decisions, and a ruinous carceral experience. Let's have a look at a few prison origin stories from challenging communities and recognize that while many in society may regard these individuals as "offenders," it's hard to disagree that they were, as well, victims.[5] While I do not quote the original text from these creative works, I encourage you to consult the cited sources because it is important to read the actual words of those whose lives were impacted. The question is, to what extent the context or environment was a critical, even determining, factor in the poor choices made, especially considering the age of the narrator, and to what extent parental behavior and community conditions and associated norms are a social or personal responsibility.

Malcolm X, in *The Autobiography of Malcolm X* (Malcolm & Haley, 1964/2015, pp. 3–22), describes his earliest memory, a night in 1929, terrorized by white men shooting at his house, which they then set afire. His youth would be shattered by domestic violence between his parents and his father beating his siblings. He recalls that most of his whippings were delivered by his mother. She eventually had a mental breakdown and was hospitalized, then treated as a mere statistic. From his experience with state social agencies, Malcolm lost mercy and compassion for a society that "will crush people, and then penalize them for not being able to stand up under the weight" (Malcolm & Haley, 1964/2015, p. 22).

Jack Henry Abbott, writing in *In the Belly of the Beast* (Abbott, 1981, pp. 6–7), recounts bouncing in and out of foster homes virtually from birth, failing to complete sixth grade, and eventually entering a reform school, after which he was sent to a penitentiary. While incarcerated he killed one prisoner and injured another, then spent as many as 15 years in solitary confinement. Abbott's own life ends badly. On parole, having demonstrated his skills as a writer with assistance from novelist Norman Mailer, he impulsively killed a waiter and, after being on the lam, returned to prison where he died by suicide, 58 years old.

Stanley Tookie Williams, in *Blue Rage, Black Redemption: A Memoir* (Williams, 2004, pp. 3–5), narrates his birth in New Orleans, born of a 17-year-old mother in poverty. His father left before Stanley turned one, leaving discipline to his mother, who devoutly used the whip in accordance with the Biblical principles of Proverbs 13.24. Williams turned to the street, where he learned that crime was economically necessary and violence a means to a preferred end. In 1969, he founded the Crips, one of the many gangs in America.[6]

Clearly, punishment as a deterrence can be futile in the context of a rational calculus of doing what is necessary to survive, regardless of the probability of consequences. Interestingly, Cesare Beccaria, writing in the 1760s, imagines the logic of a man with nothing to lose in a system of justice defined by the privileged defying even the pain of death to be the "*King of a small band of men*" exercising their unrestrained freedom and pleasure to correct the "*iniquities of fortune*" and make the establishment "*blanch and cower*" (italics in original, Beccaria, 1764, p. 69). Beccaria's account is clearly evocative of the gangs well-known to Williams. Adding further social value to his account, Williams proposes a solution to community violence, beginning with an understanding of its causes and effects, citing the absence of affordable housing, health care, quality education, secure employment, and other needs (Williams, 2004, pp. 361–362). Those truly interested in reducing the supply of people heading to prison would do well to read Williams' book and his "Protocol for Peace."

R. Dwayne Betts writes of a promising Black youth cut short in an unthinking moment at the mall in *A Question of Freedom: A Memoir of Learning, Survival, and Coming of Age in Prison* (Betts, 2009). While an honor student and junior in high school, gun in hand, he impulsively sought to relieve a white man of his car and entered the adult world of prison (p. 5).

Albert Woodfox, writing in *Solitary: Unbroken by Four Decades in Solitary Confinement: My Story of Transformation and Hope*, was born in New Orleans to a poor and illiterate, but proud woman, as was Stanley Tookie Williams (Woodfox, 2019, p. 1). His father had left. Woodfox's mom, Ruby, married a man in the Navy and moved to North Carolina. After retiring, her husband started drinking and beating her. Ruby decided to take Woodfox and his two younger brothers and flee to New Orleans, leaving behind a younger brother and sister. They lived in the poor section (p. 4), where his mother worked as a barmaid and prostitute. Woodfox stole food when finances were low, though he felt doing so was not criminal; it was survival (p. 5). In the Jim Crow era, everything was segregated. Woodfox was first called a nigger at around age 12 (p. 7). Frightened by the Klan, he stayed within the Black community, where he learned about crime on the street. There, he found that one could be a rabbit or a wolf, and he chose to be a wolf (pp. 8–9). The parallels with Stanley Tookie Williams' story are notable: Born to a 17-year-old mother in the same hospital just six years apart, the absent father, and the same rational choice to survive on the street, whether in New Orleans or Los Angeles.

Shaka Senghor, in *Writing My Wrongs: Life, Death, and Redemption in an American Prison* (Senghor, 2013/2016), recounts how his parents, once happy, grew hostile. He endured beatings from his mother until, at 14, he left (p. 30) and turned to the streets (p. 31). There he found fast money, cars, and women and built a reputation demanding acknowledgment (p. 16).

Anthony Ray Hinton, in *The Sun Does Shine: How I Found Life and Freedom on Death Row* (Hinton, 2018), shares a familiar, segregated upbringing in what was, at the time, called Bombingham, Alabama (p. 18), enduring shouts of "Nigger!" on a daily basis during his senior year in high school (p. 19). A person didn't even have to be guilty to bear the consequences of white justice in Black neighborhoods. Hinton was innocent, but he was accused of being a murderer. He was sustained in prison by visits from his childhood friend, Lester Bailey. Bryan Stevenson, founder of the Equal Justice Initiative,[7] took his case, argued it before the Supreme Court, and won a unanimous decision that freed Hinton after nearly 30 years on death row.

In *Notes of a Native Son*, James Baldwin describes a father who tried to indoctrinate James with a hatred of whites, which had a profound effect on his awareness that his own hatred could easily precipitate his demise, regardless of what white people might do to him (Baldwin, 1949/1998, pp. 63–72). Baldwin escaped to Paris when he was 24. During his first year in Paris, he was arrested and put in jail for eight days for being in possession of a hotel bedsheet stolen by a friend of his. During imprisonment, living with French cellies, he had ample time to reflect on the nature of the French in contrast to his own countrymen. On the day his case was dismissed, the story of the stolen bedsheet was received by those in the courtroom with great amusement.

Baldwin recounts how the laughter in court was at the expense of those who felt real pain in life; that this laughter was universal and would be eternal (p. 116).

These excerpts illustrate notable outcomes for some born into deprivation. We now turn to selected anthologies.

Studies and Collections

Cultural scholar H. Bruce Franklin's book, *Prison Literature in America: The Victim as Criminal and Artist* (Franklin, 1978/1989), is a groundbreaking initiative to increase our understanding of the United States by examining the role of its prisons. To do so, he considers literature ranging from British convict colonies, to African-American slavery, to the modern penitentiary, and into the period of the contemporary prison (pp. xi–xii). The 1989 edition expands his coverage from the 1978 edition with a valuable, annotated bibliography of 893 works published by American prisoners and ex-prisoners from 1798 to 1988, excluding oral works and journals published within prisons.

Ten years later, Franklin published an anthology consisting of representative samples of 20th-century prison writing in America (1998), covering in his introduction a brief history of the American prison and the renaissance of prison writing with an audience to match. Featured writers include Jack London, Kate Richards O'Hare, Etheridge Knight, Carolyn Baxter, Jerome Washington, and Mumia Abu-Jamal, among many others.

Joseph Bruchac, who taught writing in Arizona State Prison with Richard Shelton, edited a collection of poetry, *The Light from Another Country: Poetry from American Prisons*, written by 60 writers serving time in various prisons around the country (Bruchac, 1984). In his Foreword, Bruchac notes that profit motivates some prison residents to write novels, but there is no such motivation to write poems (p. xvi).

In *Are Prisons Obsolete?*, her book advocating prison abolishment, Angela Y. Davis includes a chapter on the role of gender in structuring the prison system, citing several women who have contributed to prison writing (Davis, 2003). Elsewhere in her book, she discusses prison writing, referencing an anthology she edited with Bettina Aptheker, *If They Come in the Morning*, as well as writers in the 1970s following the publication of this anthology (p. 55).

In 2005, D. Quentin Miller writes in his collection of essays, *Prose and Cons*, that at least five anthologies of prison writing were published in the prior decade, including those by Bell Gale Chevigny, H. Bruce Franklin, Wally Lamb, Janine Pommy Vega, and Judith Scheffler, with more works on the way, including popular films (2005, p. 1). The essays featured in his book cover race and ethnicity, gender, ideology, and aesthetics and language. These essays, like others, contain excerpts of prison writing. As one who spends much time inside prisons teaching writing, Miller is acutely aware of the growth of the prison population alongside the popular interest in prison narratives and notes that in past centuries the public watched gruesome spectacles of public execution, while today, we "become witnesses with a moral responsibility" by reading prison writing (Miller, 2005, p. 4).

For over two decades, Hamilton College literature professor Doran Larson has been teaching people in prison how to write. Larson compiled a major collection of their non-fiction works in *Fourth City: Essays from the Prison in America*, (2013). "Fourth City" refers to the population of people in prison at that time being equivalent to the fourth largest city in the United States, *Prisonopolis* at an earlier time. The book includes 71 essays from residents in 27 states. In his introduction, Larson writes that by accepting prison narratives by witnesses, we can start dismantling the prison of social destruction and begin to remedy the American criminal justice system (p. 2).

As a follow-up to his 2013 book, Larson wrote *Inside Knowledge: Incarcerated People on the Failures of the American Prison*, an extensive account of how people in prison bear witness to the harms caused by each of the officially professed goals of prison (2024). The book includes quotes from 210 residents who submitted essays to the American Prison Writing Archive (APWA).[8] Here again, he accounts for why the incarcerated are the most qualified to bear witness to the prison, and that their narratives are required to remedy prison as an "intrinsically pathological" environment (Larson, 2024, p. 3).

Grady Hillman, in *Arts in Corrections: Thirty Years of Annotated Publications* (2023), recounts his career of engagement with lessons learned, a directory of organizations and artists that have provided education in correctional institutions, essays, poetry, and a ten-session curriculum on how to teach poetry in prisons. This is an essential distillation of experience and advice from a master educator. I had the pleasure of publishing a couple of reviews of Hillman's book (Whitman, 2024a, 2024b).

In closing this brief review of prison writing as evidence of creativity in detention, I draw attention to Doran Larson's important work with sociologist Vesla Weaver at the Johns Hopkins University to maintain and expand the APWA, an online, publicly available repository of writing submitted by people in prison, with plans to grow the program into the Prison Witness Collective, incorporating literature from other programs and placing pieces in journals and books, beyond the online database (Larson, 2024, pp. 218–219).[9]

Visual Arts

People in prison have been writing graffiti on their cell walls and making sculptures in captivity perhaps forever. One account refers to the first known illustration of the crucifixion of Christ, found on a prison wall near the Palatine Hill in Rome (Šefčić & Nišević, 2022, p. 29). Jacey Fortin, writing in the *New York Times*, reports that in 2019, the Smithsonian Institution had secured drawings by young children depicting "pain and bewilderment" while in detention by U.S. Customs and Border Control (Fortin, 2019, July 9). Perhaps some of the best sources of historical prison art can be found in published collections of such works. Here we look at several such publications.

Cellblock Visions: Prison Art in America, is, by Phyllis Kornfeld (1997). Kornfeld's primary sources include numerous people in prisons in Connecticut, Massachusetts, California, Oklahoma, and New Mexico, with additional interviews conducted with those in detention in New Hampshire, Rhode Island, Illinois, and Florida. According to her note on sources, she witnessed the creation of many of the works in the book, as well as mistreatment and injustice (p. xxv).

In his foreword to Kornfeld's book, Roger Cardinal offers a retrospective look at the history of prison art (1997). Here he notes that the earliest examples of prison art in modern times is probably from the era of the Napoleonic Wars, when from 1797 to 1815, captive French soldiers were held in prisons in England and produced many examples of folk art. One theme was public execution, masterfully depicted with small figures and a working facsimile of a tiny guillotine (p. xvi). He also notes that the prison guard encouraged such productions and helped export pieces to the outside. Cardinal lists a number of professional artists who created work while living in internment camps during World War II, including Max Ernst, Hans Bellmer, Wols (Alfred Otto Wolfgang Schulze), and Kurt Schwitters. He also notes examples of graffiti in stairwells and bathrooms at a concentration camp, with some signed, "Kajzer Max" (p. xvii).

Italian professor of psychiatry, Cesare Lombroso was, according to Cardinal, an early compiler of prison art, and German psychiatrist Hans Prizhorn (1886–1933), in his *Bildnerei der Gefangenen* ("*Artistry of Convicts*"), provided the first account of such art as a category (p. xvii). Cardinal also mentions the collections of *art brut*, or "Outsider Art," compiled by artist Jean Dubuffet, which include prison art by convicted murderer Joseph Giavarini (1877–1934), who used soft bread to shape sculptures, which he then coated with glue and paint (p. xix). Noting an incipient popular demand for prison art, Cardinal asserts that "there has developed a network of connoisseurs, collectors, dealers, and advocates of sufficient integrity to validate Prison Art as a genuine category" (Cardinal, 1997, p. xix).

The Pencil Is a Key: Drawings by Incarcerated Artists (Gilman et al., 2019), the catalog, accompanying art exhibits at The Drawing Center and Museum of Contemporary Art in Cleveland, represents over 135 works curated by Claire Gilman, Rosario Güiraldes, Laura Hoptman, Isabella Kapur, and Duncan Tomlin, with essays by Courtenay Finn, Nicole R. Fleetwood, and Valérie Rousseau. Incarceration here is loosely defined as any situation in which freedom is denied. Works cover a period from "revolutionary Paris to apartheid-era South Africa to contemporary Syria in the midst of a civil war" (Gilman et al., 2019, pp. 9–10). The curators assert that the collection provides a strong testament to human creativity under duress, "as well as for the necessity of art – in the form of drawing – to the life of every human being" (p. 11).

Marking Time: Art in the Age of Mass Incarceration, by Nicole R. Fleetwood (Fleetwood, 2020), is far more than a collection of examples of prison art. It is an exegesis of the profound impact of prison on the author and the meaning that prison art has for society. As a young Black woman growing up in Ohio, she provides a testimony to the impact prison has on loved ones and entire communities, with relatives facing arrest and detention and people suddenly disappearing and normalizing extended absences (Fleetwood, 2020, pp. xv–xvi). Fleetwood includes some 96 illustrations by incarcerated people, including classical artist George Anthony Morton, about whom a film has been made (see the link in the Resources appendix). Her extensive narrative in the form of seven chapters provides a depth of analysis and appreciation that makes the accompanying artwork far more meaningful. In words paraphrased here, she notes that from the examples in her book, we recognize a society that employs punitive confinement to address manifold crises, but that carceral solutions, like concentration camps, have bitter outcomes only "inasmuch as we allow them to" (Fleetwood, 2020, p. 19).

Speaking of concentration camps, the United States held Japanese Americans in detention camps during World War II, and these camps witnessed a flowering of sorts of art among the detainees. As Rebecca Carballo writes in the *New York Times*, three such artists, Hisako Hibi, Miki Hayakawa, and Miné Okubo created works of art that are now getting the recognition they deserve (Carballo, 2024, April 5). As of this writing, their art is touring the country in a traveling exhibition called "Pictures of Belonging," which will be visiting the Utah Museum of Fine Arts in Salt Lake City, the Smithsonian American Art Museum in Washington, DC, the Pennsylvania Academy of the Fine Arts in Philadelphia, the Monterey Museum of Art in Monterey, California, and the Japanese American National Museum in Los Angeles, completing the tour in 2026. The article also notes that an art school started by detainees served hundreds of residents through classes in still-life and architectural drawing.

An example of contemporary artistic studies of prisons in Europe, including a chapter on art education in prison, is *Arts of Freedom: A Collection of Practices and Ideas on Art in Prison: Manual for Artists*, a project supported by the European Commission (Šefčić & Nišević, 2022). This source would have value to those interested in the possibilities of creating art in prison as well as for a possible cross-national comparative analysis of practices.

Another notable contemporary example to include here is the first-ever venue of a women's prison in Venice for the 2024 Venice Biennale, a major display of new art (Povoledo, 2024, April 28). According to reporter Elisabetta Povoledo, the curators selected a number of artists to work with women residents to create art located in the prison complex, which was visited by Pope Francis, known for his concern for the inclusion of marginalized people.

Music

Journalist Maurice Chammah, writing about American prison music, notes that the path to changing prison culture can be paved with the sounds of music (Chammah, 2023). In this chapter, I list a few examples of people or groups who are known or presumed to have created music while in detention or who were inspired by the experience. Some might be surprising.

In 1717, when German composer Johann Sebastian Bach was 22, he took a position as kapellmeister (choirmaster) at the court of Prince Leopold of Anhalt-Köthen. But he had neglected to follow the rules for departing his prior employment under Duke Wilhelm Ernst of Saxe-Weimar, who put Bach in detention, some say "imprisoned," for about a month.[10] It's hard to imagine Bach sitting idly in isolation for seven weeks. It is said that he began to compose the Well-Tempered Clavier or his Orgelbüchlein (little organ book) during that period.[11]

At age 50 or 51, Ludwig von Beethoven, seriously deaf at the time, was arrested and briefly put in jail for charges believed to be vagrancy in 1820 or 1821. He was composing sonatas at the time, and while there is no evidence he produced anything behind bars, it would not be unreasonable to suppose that he might have conceived a musical bar or two while contemplating his predicament.

British composer and suffragette Dame Ethel Smyth was 72 in 1930 when she composed The Prison, a vocal symphony. Some years earlier, in 1912, she was a member of the Women's Social and Political Union and was sentenced to two months in Holloway Prison for throwing stones at a house during a suffrage demonstration. She was released three weeks later, but while imprisoned had organized a performance of her vocal work, March of the Women. Clearly, the experience made a resounding impression on her (Wood, 2020).

In 1937, American composer Henry Cowell was imprisoned at San Quentin State Prison for 15 years on morals charges, reminiscent of Oscar Wilde in England some 42 years earlier. During his period in prison, he created 60 compositions.

Journalist Maurice Chammah (cited earlier), writing for The Marshall Project, provides a note on American prison music since the 1930s when a Texas prison featured a weekly radio show that may have reached five million (Chammah, 2023). A group of residents in a Tennessee facility sang doo-wop as The Prisoners and were permitted to record their music at Sun Studio in Memphis. Chammah also highlights the prison recording work of Die Jim Crow, today known as FREER Records, described later in this book. One of Chammah's sources is *Texas Jailhouse Music: A Prison Band History* (Caroline Gnagy, 2016).

Collections of prisoner work songs recorded in the South during the Jim Crow era are quite unique as a genre and have a plaintive beauty to them that belies the dreadful and deadly conditions from which they emerged.

Musicologist Alan Lomax, born in Austin, Texas, in 1915, traveled the country from 1933 to into the 1990s recording folk musicians in the South, Southwest, Midwest, Northeast, Haiti, and the Bahamas.[12] In 1947, Lomax recorded songs at Parchman Farm, the Mississippi State Penitentiary. He compiled and recorded works for both scholarly and commercial purposes and promoted his recordings, including those of himself, on commercially produced records and radio. The Library of Congress produced a compilation of over 250 of his productions made between 1943 and 2016 (Campbell et al., 2016). The website devoted to Lomax and his legacy notes that he considered these prison songs as "among the world's great music."[13] Lomax died in 2002.

The Smithsonian Institution also has a collection of "Negro Prison Camp Worksongs" recorded by Pete and Toshi Seeger at two Texas prison farms in 1951[14] and "Prison Worksongs" recorded by Dr. Harry Oster at state penitentiaries in Louisiana in the late 1950s.[15] The Smithsonian attributes the origins of these songs to the prisoners' West African ancestry and the era of slavery in America.

Finally, Benjamin Harbert provides a masterful account of prison music since the late 19th century from one of the nation's most notorious prisons in *Instrument of the State: A Century of Music in Louisiana's Angola Prison* (Harbert, 2023).

▪ ▪ ▪

These accounts of examples of creativity drawn from literature, visual arts, and music clearly attest to creativity in prison. I now turn to evidence drawn from current creators at work.

Notes

1 See: www.loc.gov/classroom-materials/immigration/japanese/behind-the-wire/, cited 26 February 2024.

2 See: https://benton.uconn.edu/2008/01/22/the-art-of-gaman-arts-and-crafts-from-the-japanese-american-internment-camps-1942–1946/, cited 26 February 2024.

3 See: https://encyclopedia.densho.org/Literature_in_camp/, cited 26 February 2024. Other books also describe the experience of living in American internment camps, but, as Peter Suzuki writes in the Introduction, "no other author can claim to have written this form of literature during the camp days" (Nakamura, 1996, p. no page number).

4 See, for example: https://developingchild.harvard.edu/media-coverage/take-the-ace-quiz-and-learn-what-it-does-and-doesnt-mean/, cited 23 April 2024.

5 See *The House I Live In* (Jarecki, 2012), www.youtube.com/watch?v=vWToa5bOeI8, cited 21 February 2024.

6 See: https://en.wikipedia.org/wiki/Gangs_in_the_United_States, cited 19 July 2024.

7 See: https://eji.org/, Cited 16 February 2024.
8 To view how to submit essays, see the Call for Essays at https://prisonwitness.org/how-to-submit/.
9 See: https://prisonwitness.org/, cited 17 September 2023.
10 See: www.bach-leipzig.de/en/neutral/johann-sebastian-bach-%E2%94%80-chronology, cited 16 February 2024.
11 See: www.dw.com/en/300-years-of-johann-sebastian-bachs-well-tempered-clavier/a-62188220, cited 16 February 2024.
12 See: www.culturalequity.org/alan-lomax/about-alan, cited 25 February 2024.
13 See previous reference and: www.culturalequity.org/, cited 25 February 2024.
14 See: https://folkways.si.edu/negro-prison-camp-worksongs/african-american-music-folk/album/smithsonian, cited 25 February 2024.
15 See: https://folkways.si.edu/prison-worksongs/blues/music/album/smithsonian, cited 25 February 2024.

References

Abbott, J. H. (1981). *In the belly of the beast.* Vintage Books.

Ashton, S.-A. (2023). *Pathways to adolescent male violent offending.* Routledge.

Baldwin, J. (1949/1998). *Notes of a native son.* Library Classics of the United States.

Baldwin, J. (1962/1998). *The fire next time.* Literary Classics of the United States.

Beccaria, C. (1764). The death penalty. In R. Bellamy (Ed.), *Beccaria: On crimes and punishments and other writings* (pp. 66–72). Cambridge University Press.

Bernstein, J. M. (Ed.). (1965). *Baudelaire Rimbaud Verlaine: Selected verse and prose poems.* The Citadel Press.

Betts, R. D. (2009). *A question of freedom: A memoir of learning, survival, and coming of age in prison.* Penguin Group.

Broadhead, J. (2006). *Unlocking the prison muse: The inspirations and effects of prisoners' writing in Britain.* Cambridge Academic.

Brower, R. (1999). Dangerous minds: Eminently creative people who spent time in jail. *Creativity Research Journal, 12*(1), 3–13.

Bruchac, J. (Ed.). (1984). *The light from another country: Poetry from American prisons.* The Greenfield Review Press.

Campbell, L., Harvey, T., Warman, B., Willer, C., & Wogan, H. (2016). *Alan Lomax discography.* American Folklife Center, Library of Congress. www.loc.gov/static/collections/alan-lomax-manuscripts/documents/Lomax_discography_master.pdf cited 25 February 2024.

Carballo, R. (2024, April 5). Women who made art in Japanese internment camps are getting their due. *The New York Times.* www.nytimes.com/2024/04/05/arts/hayakawa-hibi-okubo-japanese-art-exhibit.html cited 5 April 2024.

Cardinal, R. (1997). Foreword: A brief history of prison art. In P. Kornfeld (Ed.), *Cellblock visions: Prison art in America* (pp. xiii–xxi). Princeton University Press.

Carnochan, W. B. (1995). The literature of confinement. In N. Morris & D. J. Rothman (Eds.), *The Oxford history of the prison: The practice of punishment in western society* (pp. 381–406). Oxford University Press.

Chammah, M. (2023, August 3). Redemption songs: The forgotten history of American prison music. *The Marshall Project*. www.themarshallproject.org/2023/08/03/prison-music-songs-history-rehabilitation-redemption cited 17 February 2024.

Davidson, J., & King, E. (Eds.). (2023). *Rattling the cages: Oral histories of North American political prisoners*. AK Press.

Davis, A. Y. (2003). *Are prisons obsolete?* Seven Stories Press.

De Grazia, S. (1994). *Machiavelli in hell*. Vintage Books.

Douglass, F. (1857). *Two speeches by Fredericl Douglass; one on West India emancipation, delivered at Canandaigua, Aug. 4th, and the other on the Dred Scott Decision, delivered in New York on the occasion of the anniversary of the American Abolition Society, May, 1857*. C. P. Dewey, Printer.

Felitti, V. J., Anda, R. F., Nordenberg, D., Williamson, D. F., Spitz, A. M., Edwards, V., Koss, M. P., & Marks, J. S. (1998). Relationship of childhood abuse and household dysfunction to many of the leading causes of death in adults: The Adverse Childhood Experiences (ACE) study. *American Journal of Preventive Medicine*, *14*(4), 245–258. www.ajpmonline.org/article/S0749-3797(98)00017-8/fulltext cited 10 April 2024.

Fleetwood, N. R. (2020). *Marking time: Art in the age of mass incarceration*. Harvard University Press.

Fortin, J. (2019, July 9). Drawings by migrant children in Texas catch the Smithsonian's eye. *The New York Times*. www.nytimes.com/2019/07/09/us/smithsonian-migrant-children-drawings.html cited 8 March 2024.

Franklin, H. B. (1978/1989). *Prison literature in America: The victim as criminal and artist, expanded edition*. Oxford University Press.

Franklin, H. B. (Ed.). (1998). *Prison writing in 20th century America*. Penguin Books.

Gilman, C., Güiraldes, R., Hoptman, L., Kapur, I., & Tomlin, D. (2019). *The pencil is a key: Drawings by incarcerated artists*. The Drawing Center.

Graf, G. H.-J., Chihuri, S., Blow, M., & Li, G. (2021). Adverse childhood experiences and justice system contact: A systematic review. *Pediatrics*, *147*(1), 13. https://doi.org/10.1080/09546553.2020.1767604

Gramsci, A. (1971/2003). *Selections from the prison notebooks, 1929–1935*. International Publishers.

Harbert, B. J. (2023). *Instrument of the state: A century of music in Louisiana's Angola Prison*. Oxford University Press.

Hillman, G. (2023). *Arts in corrections: Thirty years of annotated publications*. Routledge.

Hinton, A. R. (2018). *The sun does shine: How I found life and freedom on death row*. St. Martin's Press.

Jarecki, E. (2012). *The house I live in*. Abramorama. www.youtube.com/watch?v=vWToa5bOeI8 cited 21 February 2024.

Kerman, P. (2011). *Orange is the new black: My year in a women's prison.* Spiegel & Grau, Random House.
Kornfeld, P. (1997). *Cellblock visions: Prison art in America.* Princeton University Press.
Larson, D. (Ed.). (2013). *Fourth city: Essays from the prison in America.* Michigan State University Press.
Larson, D. (2024). *Inside knowledge: Incarcerated people on the failures of the American prison.* New York University Press.
Machiavelli, N. (1532/2008). *The prince.* Oxford University Press.
Manduca, R., & Sampson, R. J. (2021). Childhood exposure to polluted neighborhood environments and intergenerational income mobility, teenage birth, and incarceration in the USA. *Population and Environment, 42*, 501–523. https://doi.org/10.1007/s11111-020-00371-5
Miller, D. Q. (Ed.). (2005). *Prose and cons.* McFarland & Company, Inc., Publishers.
Murphy, A. R. (2015). The emergence of William Penn, 1668–1671. *Journal of Church and State, 57*(2, Spring), 333–359. https://doi-org.ezp-prod1.hul.harvard.edu/10.1093/jcs/cst144
Nakamura, H. (1996). *Treadmill.* Mosaic Press.
Neier, A. (1995/1998). Confining dissent: The political prison. In N. Morris & D. J. Rothman (Eds.), *The Oxford history of prison: The practice of punishment in Western society* (pp. 350–380). Oxford University Press.
Paxton, R. O. (2004). *The anatomy of fascism.* Vintage Books.
Pellico, S. (1836). *My prisons, memoirs of Silvio Pellico of Saluzzo.* Charles Folsom.
Perrottet, T. (2015, February). Who was the Marquis de Sade? Even in the age of Fifty Shades of Grey, the 18th-century libertine is as shocking as ever. *Smithsonian Magazine.* www.smithsonianmag.com/history/who-was-marquis-de-sade-180953980/?all cited 17 May 2024.
Peters, E. M. (1995). Prison before the prison. In N. Morris & D. J. Rothman (Eds.), *The Oxford history of the prison: The practice of punishment in Western society* (pp. 3–43). Oxford University Press.
Povoledo, E. (2024, April 28). Pope's visit to art exhibition in prison is a first for Venice Biennale. *The New York Times.* www.nytimes.com/2024/04/28/world/europe/venice-biennale-prison-vatican-pope.html cited 28 April 2024.
Šefčić, M., & Nišević, A. J. (Eds.). (2022). *Arts of freedom: A collection of practices and ideas on art in prison, manual for artists.* Croatian Association of Fine Artists.
Senghor, S. (2013/2016). *Writing my wrongs: Life, death, and redemption in an American prison.* Convergent Books.
Spierenburg, P. (1995/1998). The body and the state: Early modern Europe. In N. Morris & D. J. Rothman (Eds.), *The Oxford history of the prison* (pp. 44–70). Oxford University Press.
Thoreau, H. D. (1849–1863/1993). *Civil disobedience and other essays.* Dover Publications, Inc.
Whitman, J. R. (2024a). Documenting a lifetime of prison arts [book review]. *UNESCO International Review of Education.* https://doi.org/10.1007/s11159-024-10064-y

Whitman, J. R. (2024b). Testimony of a prison arts evangelist [book review]. *Journal of Criminal Justice Education*. https://doi.org/10.1080/10511253.2024.2306812

Williams, S. T. (2004). *Blue rage, black redemption: A memoir*. Simon & Schuster.

Willsher, K. (2015, October 17). How 555 nights in jail helped to make Paul Verlaine a 'prince of poets'. *The Observer*. www.theguardian.com/books/2015/oct/18/paul-verlaine-new-exhibition-mons cited 20 June 2024.

Windisch, S., Simi, P., Blee, K., & DeMichele, M. (2022). Measuring the extent and nature of Adverse Childhood Experiences (ACE) among former white supremacists. *Terrorism and Political Violence*, *34*(6), 1207–1228. https://doi.org/10.1080/09546553.2020.1767604

Wood, E. (2020). Smyth: The prison. In *Dame Ethel Smyth: The prison* (pp. 11–13). Chandos Records Ltd.

Woodfox, A. (2019). *Solitary: Unbroken by four decades in solitary confinement. My story of transformation and hope*. Grove Press.

X, M., & Haley, A. (1964/2015). *The autobiography of Malcolm X*. Ballantine Books.

5 Creators at Work

The foregoing evidence of creativity that has emerged in carceral contexts is impressive. There are instances of individuals who had already achieved artistic ability prior to incarceration, and we would have been at a loss if their creative work had been prevented or destroyed while in detention. Sadly, there are cases in which prison authorities have confiscated and destroyed creative works. There are cases in which individuals who discovered the value of the arts once inside continued producing following release. Still others may have found that engagement in writing, visual arts, or music while incarcerated simply provided a way to endure an otherwise deadening existence without leaving any traces of work.

There is, perhaps, no better way to argue for the social value of creativity born in prison than to provide current examples of people in prison actually producing creative works and testifying to the benefits of doing so for themselves and others. Photographer Peter Merts compiled a collection of images taken of creative residents in the California correctional system in his book, *Ex Crucible: The Passion of Incarcerated Artists* (Merts, 2022). His images and the stories shared by his subjects exemplify what is possible. Seeing works created in prison, face-to-face, is particularly compelling, as I experienced in Lincoln's Cottage. The Visualizing Abolition and Seeing Through Stone exhibitions at the Institute of the Arts and Sciences at the University of California at Santa Cruz were also exemplary initiatives to bring examples of visual and musical arts directly to the public.[1]

To offer new examples of creators currently or recently incarcerated, I solicited a number of people in prison known to be engaged in writing, the visual arts, and music. I wanted to learn their stories and experience their art, if possible. Indeed, everyone in detention has a story to tell. As Yale English professor Caleb Smith, a specialist in prison writing, puts it: the defendant, denied the opportunity to tell his or her full story during the investigation and trial, may now, in prison, take the opportunity to tell the story (Kilgannon, 2024, February 18). Not everyone contacted was willing or able to respond. Prison journalist John J. Lennon, for example, who wrote a thoughtful piece reflecting on his crimes in *The Washington Post* (2019), was not able to

DOI: 10.4324/9781003566021-6

contribute to this project, though he kindly nominated two other writers who did respond.

Appendix B describes my approach to seeking stories. Altogether, I received 12 replies, including ten men and two women. All but one were incarcerated as I began my study; one was released during my study. Eleven are in state prisons, of which one is a private, for-profit facility; one is in a federal prison. The prisons range in security classifications: low (1), medium (6), maximum (3), and supermaximum (1). Eight of the ten indicated that they had been previously incarcerated. Of those currently incarcerated, the number of years of total incarceration ranged from 3 to 30, with an average of 17 years.

Birth years ranged from 1967 to 1993, with an average of 1981. Ages ranged from 31 to 57, with an average of 43. One was adopted; two were veterans. Ten indicated having access to a library inside, but few of them reported it to be of use to them. Only three of 12 reported understanding how to register a copyright. All but two reported having a family member or other contact on the outside who could represent their financial and legal interests. All were willing to be contacted for follow-up queries. One respondent engages only in music, and three only in art. The others report engaging in multiple artistic disciplines: literature, visual arts, and/or music.

In addition to this sample of 12 respondents, I include art examples from an additional six artists and samples of musical works created by nine additional musicians for whom I do not have data to supplement the statistics above. The states represented by the 27 creators in all groups are: California, Colorado, Illinois, Iowa, Kansas, Maine, Maryland, New Jersey, New York, North Carolina, Ohio, Oklahoma, Pennsylvania, South Carolina, Texas, and Virginia.

With the exception of musicians, who were not included in my study, most respondents to my research queries provided substantive responses for my research purposes. All quotations are used with permission. To round out this section on working creators, I have also added examples of artwork posted on the Justice Arts Coalition (JAC) website. Selecting work is often difficult because since people in prison do not have easy access to new subject matter, they often make copies of works from sources like magazines. This presents a potential copyright problem, so for the publication, it's best to pass over works that are not original to the creators, in the public domain, or past the copyright expiration. The works here appear in alphabetical order by the artist's name or pseudonym. Note that due to difficulties in obtaining high-resolution digital images of artwork, some selections may appear to be of poor quality.

For many other examples of arts in detention by currently or recently incarcerated individuals, see the PEN America's Prison and Justice Writing site (https://pen.org/prison-writing/), JAC for examples of visual arts (https://thejusticeartscoalition.org/), and FREER Records for music recordings (www.freerrecords.com/).

Cedar Annenkovna, Colorado

Born during the Soviet withdrawal from Azerbaijan in 1987, artist and muralist Cedar Annenkovna, a Shia Muslim, resides in a for-profit, maximum-security prison in Denver, Colorado. Incarcerated more than once, she has been in detention for seven years and five months to date.[2]

Annenkovna enjoys writing poetry, fiction, and journalism and has written many long essays. Her visual arts employ any medium – airbrush, paint, graphite, ink, coffee or "whatever is available." She also practices spoken word with music. Annenkovna's talent is appreciated at her facility. She has been permitted to create many murals, including a large wall mural in the entrance foyer to the program center at the facility so everyone passing through can see and appreciate her work. In her words,

> I love nothing more in here than to take these blank austere white walls and liberate them with the intention of breathing life – vitality inspiration and hope into this place with the murals I create. I'm grateful that I have been granted the liberties to do so in here.

Annenkovna's words speak to the public importance of art in detention and the need for recognizing ownership of creations:

> A prisoner might tap into this same energy and produce some amazing things. This process of creative innovation and liberty should never be inhibited regardless of what shackles may be placed on the physical body.

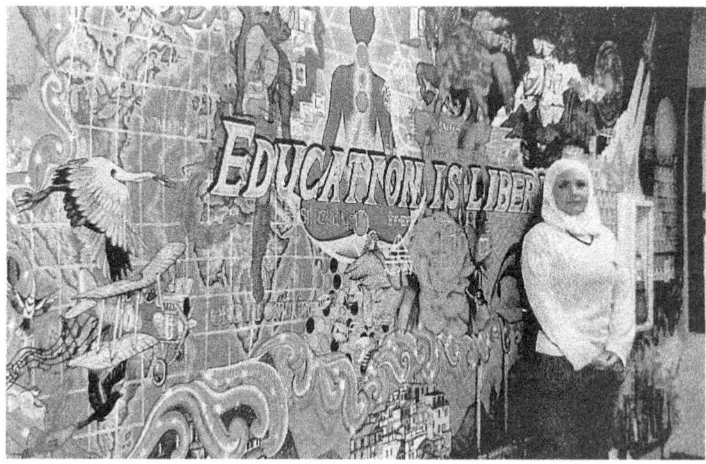

Figure 5.1 Education is liberation, by Cedar Annenkovna, courtesy of the artist.

Art in its many forms is a public service and a very necessary stand that forms the fiber of the societies and communities we exist in. Yes by all means creative works from wherever they are derived should be made available and accessible to and by the public. It is important that ownership of such creations should remain with the creator because this is what allows us to recognize beauty and individuality. I do not want to be recognized as a prison-incarcerated artist. My ability to create and innovate expands beyond these perimeters. I am Cedar Annenkovna.

Rayfel Bell, Virginia

Artist Rayfel Bell, who signs his work "R. Zumar," was born in 1982 and is originally from Petersburg, Virginia, a small city south of Richmond. He grew up surrounded by drugs and theft. After being released from a first conviction, he linked up with a friend from El Salvador and ended up with a charge that would send him back until 2062. I discovered Bell's art at The Lincoln Cottage exhibit. I purchased a watercolor that I felt exemplified a resident's aspiration to recreate him or herself during the time spent in detention. I chose Bell's self-portrait, "Bohemia," with his permission, for the frontispiece of this book because I feel it conveys a profound message at the heart of this book, that regardless of one's past, one can envision and strive to become a better person. Bell himself exemplifies that ambition.

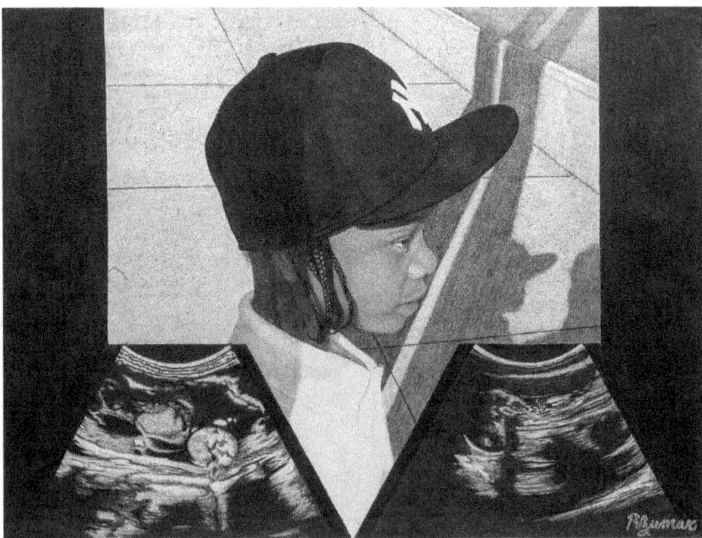

Figure 5.2 Motivation, by R. Zumar, courtesy of the artist.

My wife purchased another piece by R. Zumar, *Motivation*, which conveys the promise of a young boy situated in his neighborhood, framed by what appear to be ultrasound images of him in his mother's womb. Both of these works conjure the essential questions about life starting with, "What if . . . ," questions worth reflection during incarceration.

In addition to creating art, Bell has written and published a book on science fiction, *Tales of Vrenarri: Red Summer* (Bell, 2020). More work by Bell, listed as R. Zumar, can be found on the JAC website: https://thejusticeartscoalition.org/portfolio/r-zumar/.

Jaiquan Fayson, New York

Artist Jaiquan Fayson is 41 years old at the time of our conversation. He was first incarcerated at age 16 and has been in and out a number of times. He describes how artists would use any available materials – soap, sheets,

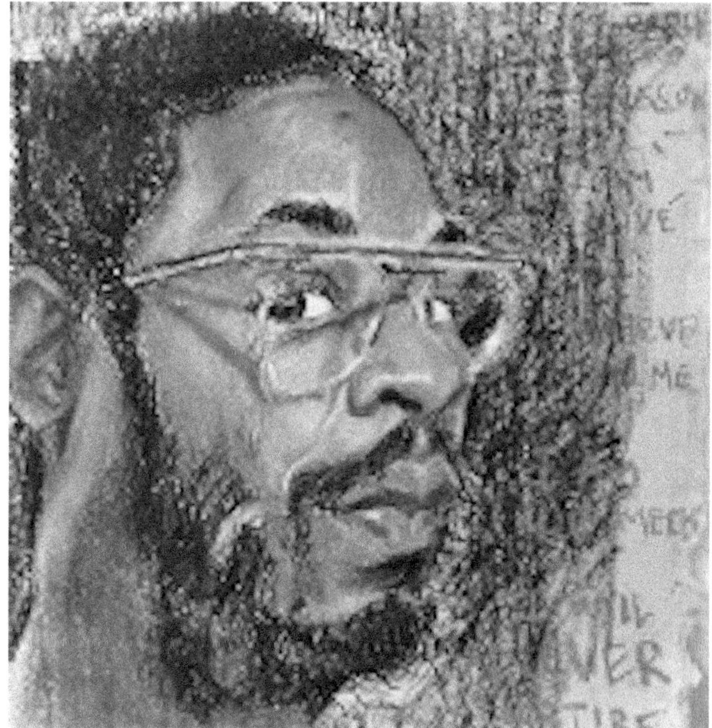

Figure 5.3 Self-portrait 2014, by Jaiquan Fayson, courtesy of the artist.

handkerchiefs – to sculpt and draw. Because these were state-issued materials, such use was not permitted and if caught, the artwork would be confiscated. A legal pad and pen were his only materials; "I don't remember seeing a sketchbook anywhere in the prison."

Fayson referred me to a short film made about his experience called, *Drawing Freedom*, produced in 2019 by The Healthy US Collaborative.[3] In the film, Fayson recounts how he felt alone as a child and grew up without a father. His youth was spent living in poverty in Bedford-Stuyvesant, a part of Brooklyn, New York. He felt he had no value. Seeing flashy gold chains and nice clothes made an impression. In prison, Fayson experienced solitary confinement but found a soothing effect and a means for self-reflection through drawing. Art, Fayson says, changed his life and gave him a sense of value. Following his release, he is now committed to being there for his own son.

Fayson's artwork can be viewed on his website: www.jaiquanfayson.com/

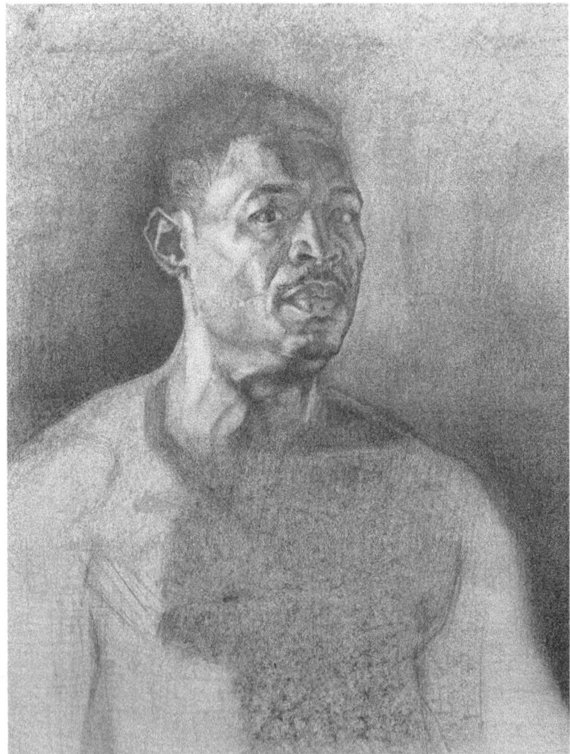

Figure 5.4 Self-portrait 2024, by Jaiquan Fayson, courtesy of the artist.

FloGriffin, South Carolina

Rapper FloGriffin was born in Baltimore, Maryland, in 1976, and raised in Annapolis. He is serving his current sentence, not his first, at a state facility in South Carolina. He's been incarcerated for 25 of his 48 years, or just over half his life so far. His parents were from the small town of Davidsonville, Maryland, and both eventually became addicted and dependent on drugs. He never knew them very well and they passed away while he was incarcerated. FloGriffin writes that his criminal activity started early due to the family's poverty:

> My life of crime started before [his parents' addiction]. I caught my first charge at eight years old for stealing a dingy boat from the downtown harbor. Not having anything, but desiring everything I seen others with made stealing my only way of getting whatever I wanted. This included clothing, food, etc. . . . I came up poor, but I don't think I could understand what poverty was because in the 80s everyone was poor and it was an accepted and unchallenged fact of life.

Gangs were not an influence because they were unknown to the youth in Annapolis at the time. FloGriffin reports learning of gangs in his 30s. Long before then, he discovered rap while incarcerated. As of this writing, FloGriffin has one more year to release. An example of his hip-hop imagination appears in the box (reproduced with permission).

Box 5.1 Dead Beat, by FloGriffin, circa 2004–2005

Hook

I never ment to hurt you
I never ment to make you cry
I never ment to leave you all alone
Leave you on your own
Without me home by your side.

Verse 1:

When you look me in my eyes
You'll see your eyes looking back at you
Asking you daddy did you love me.
Why didn't you hug me in the morning before I went to school
And tell me where you were when I turned two and got my first tooth

I wanted you to see me last Christmas when I got my new shoes
And this clown dude that's with Mommy
Got me a pair of pink boots
He be telling me that he love me
But it ain't the truth
Cause I know that he ain't you
Damn it I wish I was with you!
Sorry about the cursing
But I'm hurting searching for the answer
How can I look exactly like you but you treat me like a stranger
I got all of your letters
And I would have wrote you back
But I couldn't read or write yet
I had just taken my first steps
Why don't Mommy bring me to see you
She be acting like she hate you
But I know she still loves you
She got pictures & some tapes of you
That she plays when it rains
Staring at your name
Granma told her that you've changed
But she holding on to pain
Why don't they let you go
Ma' say I ain't old enough to know
But how old do you gotta be to know
You love somebody you don't know
I pray to God every night
But She don't be answering my crys
You said to keep hope alive
But hope is killing me inside
I seen uncle Jamal the other day
He said to tell you hi
And aunt Michelle was getting high
What does he mean by getting high
He had some funny eyes
They was red like fire was inside 'em
Then when Mommy wasn't looking he put money in my pockets
Well I gotta go write me back as soon as you get this
And send some pictures
With hugs and kisses
Love you, Princess

Hook

Verse 2:

I remember the first time I saw you
I wanted to hold you close and talk with you
Walk with you through the awkward events
That life would offer you
If part of you is a part of me
Then I'm special
I know I wasn't the best example
But you were a handle
I just couldn't handle
I couldn't handle being a man to your mother
How I'm a father you
I ain't making excuses
I'm useless
It's sad but it's true
I'm glad that you well
Right now I'm trapped inside of hell
Locked inside of a cell
Writing this letter with a heart swell
Cause I'm sorry I failed you
Sorry I wasn't there to raise you
But I was chasing a dream
With a scheme that made me hateful
This life of mine is a crime an I'm a die to remain faithful
You better off without me
Than with me
How is it you can't remember me
But can't forget me
How you forgiving so merciful
Wanting to get personal
With this nigger that's hurting you
I don't deserve you
I ain't worthy to speak a word to you
You are the gift the God blessed me with
And I deserted you
How old are you now
You gotta man
He better bow down
And honor you for the Queen that you are

Or catch a beat down
I guess it's too late to be a father now
I'm a call next week
Be there to accept
And here are some pictures of me
Peace
Love daddy . . .

Hook

Verse 3:

"Hello, you have a collect call from . . .
To accept this call press one . . .

Princess speaking:
Hello daddy, dad is that you
I can't believe I'm talking to you
So many tears so many years I needed to talk to you
I got in trouble today
And Mommy took my video game away
Cause I threw dirt in this girl's hair
When the teacher was looking the other way
Daddy she was so mean to me
She made me cry with what she said to me
She told me I was ugly
And that's the reason that you left me
Say it's not true . . .

Daddy speaking:
It's not true
My princess you're beautiful
Wow you remind me of me when I was a juvenile . . .

Princess speaking:
Well tell me when you getting out
I got so much to tell you . . .

Daddy speaking:
In about three hopefully
If this devil will let go of me
But there's something about this soldier in me
That won't let him control me . . .

Princess speaking:
But I want you and I need you
Daddy, why don't you want to be with me
I needed you here when this nigga was beating Mommy
And I tried to stop him and he pushed me and kept beating Mommy
It's like every night they would fight and I would go to sleep hungry
Crying, begging, and wishing you would come and stop it
Or at least come and bet the boogie monster out the closet . . .

Operator:
You got two seconds remaining . . .

Daddy speaking:
I'm a see you soon I promise . . .

Princess speaking:
Daddy I love you . . .
– Phone disconnects –

Operator speaking:
We're sorry, if you would like to make a call please hang up and try your call again later.

Brian D. Hindson, Texas

Artist and journalist Brian D. Hindson, born in 1967, is 56 years old at this writing and will be 68 when he completes his sentence at a low-security Federal Correctional Institution in Texas 12 years from now. He was 40 when incarcerated and had spent 16 years and 2 months in detention, with no previous incarcerations, when he responded to my questions. He writes:

> I feel fortunate in that I've been able to be part of what the FBOP calls HobbyCraft and the past 16 yrs I've worked in the Recreation dept and be able to create works, help expand the programs and opportunities for others. I act very much as an advocate and liaison with staff for inmates wishing to be creative.
>
> People draw, paint, crochet, leatherwork, up-cycle chip bags into various items (picture frames, motorcycles, you name it), take trash bags – turn them into string for bracelets, necklaces, rosaries – also using pencils (the wood) a bit of paint & they can make detailed & intricate braided items. I help them get the colors (paints) they need to make

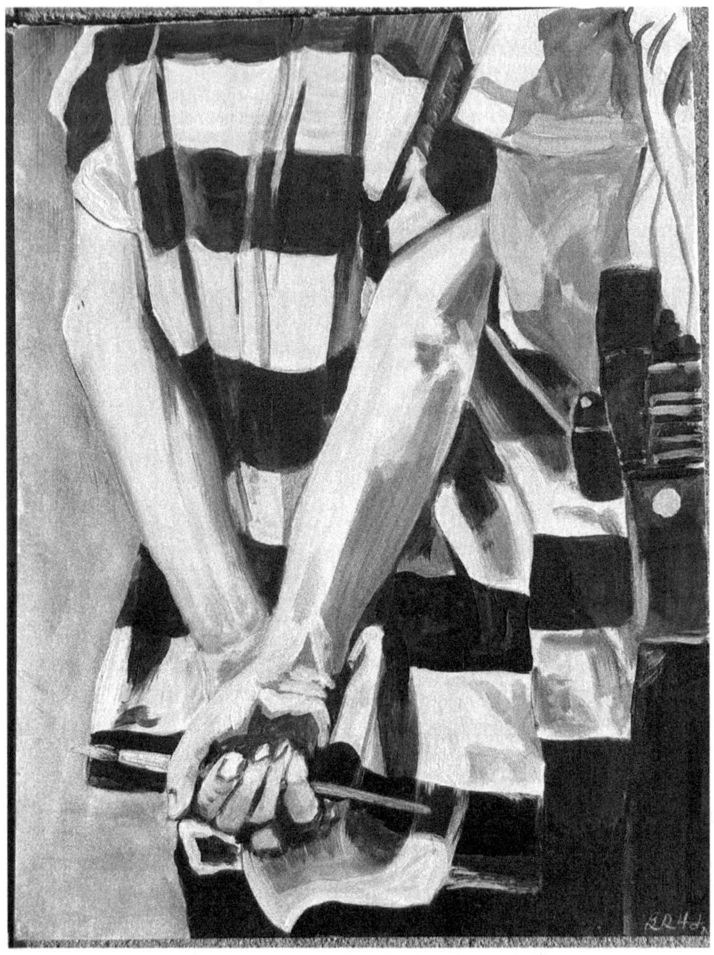

Figure 5.5 Not my brush, by Brian D. Hindson, courtesy of the artist.

different colored strings. Dream-catchers – you name it. The artistic – the creative – ALWAYS find a way – even if it's just a pen/pencil to paper.

It's a good environment (our HobbyCraft areas) – people are supportive of each other – no MATTER their crime, or background. I've seen the queerest fellow help the baddest bad-ass white boy do/learn something. It's an avenue to see others helping others & bridging gaps. I think it's a beginning to a dialogue – a common interest – for people in here as well as in/out of prison.

I have visual work at Justice Arts Coalition, written/visual work at Prison Journalism Project and various other journals/sites . . .. It's against BOP

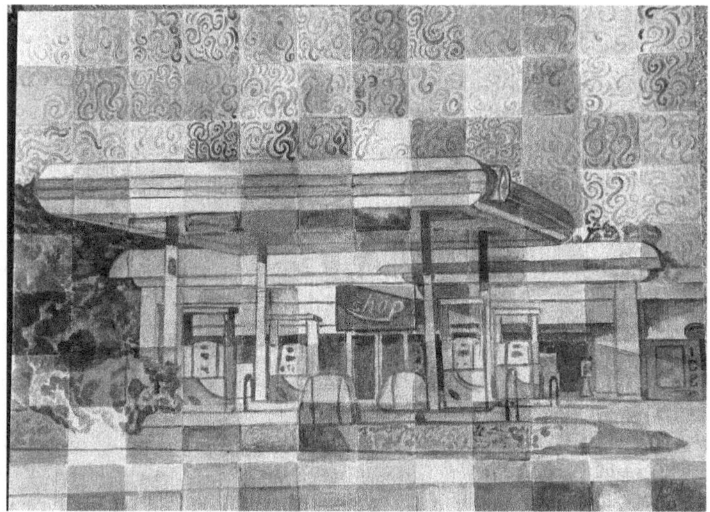

Figure 5.6 BP gas station, by Brian D. Hindson, courtesy of the artist.

> policy for me to sell my works directly. But I can receive honorariums, or a friend/family member can receive payment . . .. I hope people see my work as contributing some way. Seeing things differently. Look past my crime.

Hindson won second place for best illustration in the 2024 Stillwater Awards, sponsored by the Society of Professional Journalists and the Prison Journalism Project (PJP). As a final note, Hindson shares, "I believe ARTS can help so many people connect with not only others – but maybe even themselves."

Additional works may be seen at https://thejusticeartscoalition.org/portfolio/brian-hindson/.

LaMarr W. Knox, New York

LaMarr Knox is a writer and crochet artist. Born in Kingston, New York, he was raised with two older sisters by his mother, who joined the Army after earning a master's degree. When she was stationed at Fort Bliss, she sent Knox to live with his father. His father beat him until he ran away at 13 to start a life of drug dealing and gang-banging.

Finding inspiration from those around him and mentored by incarcerated journalism legend John J. Lennon, Knox has written essays featured at The Marshall Project journalism site, including "From Crip to Crochet Artist" and "How the Police and Vigilante Killings of Black People Have Forced Me to Look Inside."[4]

Marcus "Da Mac" S. McKie, South Carolina

Marcus McKie is a hip-hop/rap artist and writer performing under the name Da Mac. He notes, "It keeps me busy and makes my time go by faster [and] also gives me a sense of accomplishment." Born in 1980 in the historically Black community of Greenview, Columbia, South Carolina, McKie recalls learning how to be a man mostly from people in the streets. His father was always working, "we hardly saw him." "I remember watching my father come in from long shifts of work and still barely able to make ends meet on payday. I told myself I never want to live like that when I grow up."

His facility has a music program that provides access to instruments. Residents learn music theory, music history, and how to play guitar, keyboards, and drums, as well as how to engineer music. Resources and computer memory are limited, and McKie feels some resistance from officials. He appreciates spending time producing music that could otherwise be spent in unproductive ways: "Allowing inmates to express their creativity keeps them from expressing it in negative ways like violence and drug use." McKie has released several songs on the "Da Massez" album; he solos on "When the Smoke Clears." He receives royalties through FREER and his family.

Chad Merrill, Virginia

Artist Chad Merrill was born in Hammond, Indiana, in 1986 and grew up in Arizona after he turned four. He is currently a resident at a state facility in Virginia. He writes:

> From the age of 8, I was in 32 different foster/group homes and 6 juvenile prisons. When I turned 15, while on the run from being on juvenile parole, I started to find my own way in the world. I still managed to find myself locked up a few more times before I was 18, but was able to take care of myself.

I first learned about Merrill's work at the art exhibit at The Lincoln Cottage. I purchased one of his works, a portrait of Alfred Hitchcock imagined with a raven emerging from the top of his head, as if Hitchcock was birthing the conception of his 1963 adrenaline-fueled avian nightmare, *The Birds*. I included this portrait as an example of art created in prison in a chapter I wrote for the *Cambridge Handbook of Intellectual Property and Social Justice* (Whitman, 2024).

Merrill was grateful for the publicity and gave me an additional piece he created (for which I compensated him), a copy of a portrait by Humphrey Bogart's mother, Maud Humphrey Bogart, on which the date 1938 appears.[5]

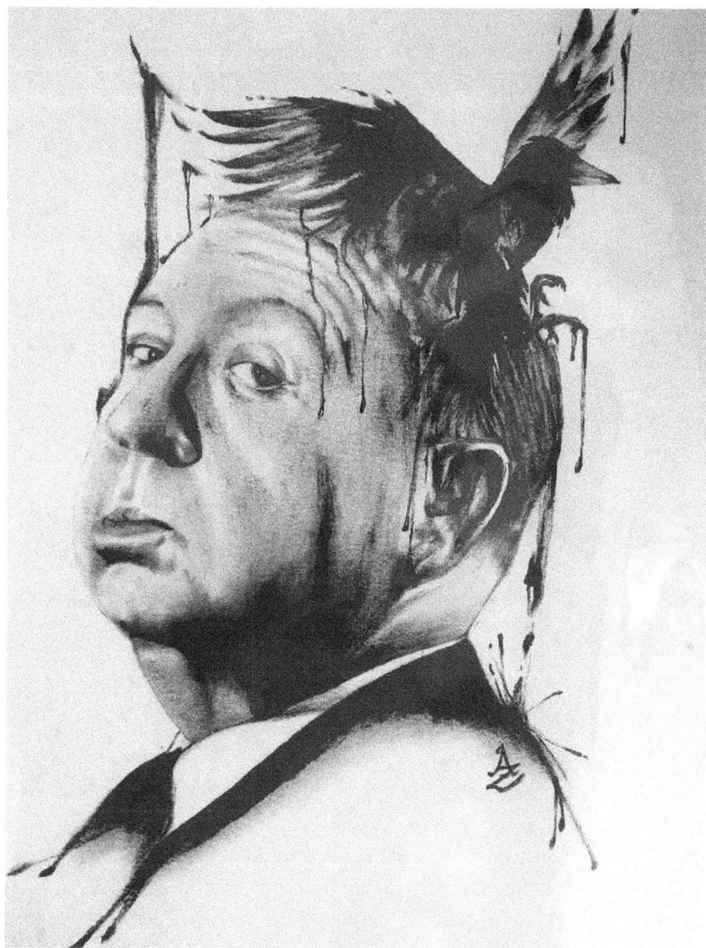

Figure 5.7 Hitchcock, by Chad Merrill, courtesy of the artist.

In February 2020, Merrill wrote me a letter, in which he describes his methods and what it means to paint, part of which reads:

> In October of 2018 I made my first homemade paint brush out of toothbrush bristles and took a shitty flex pen (3 ½ inches long and rubber) and blew out the ink into a toothpaste cap and sat down to paint portraits.

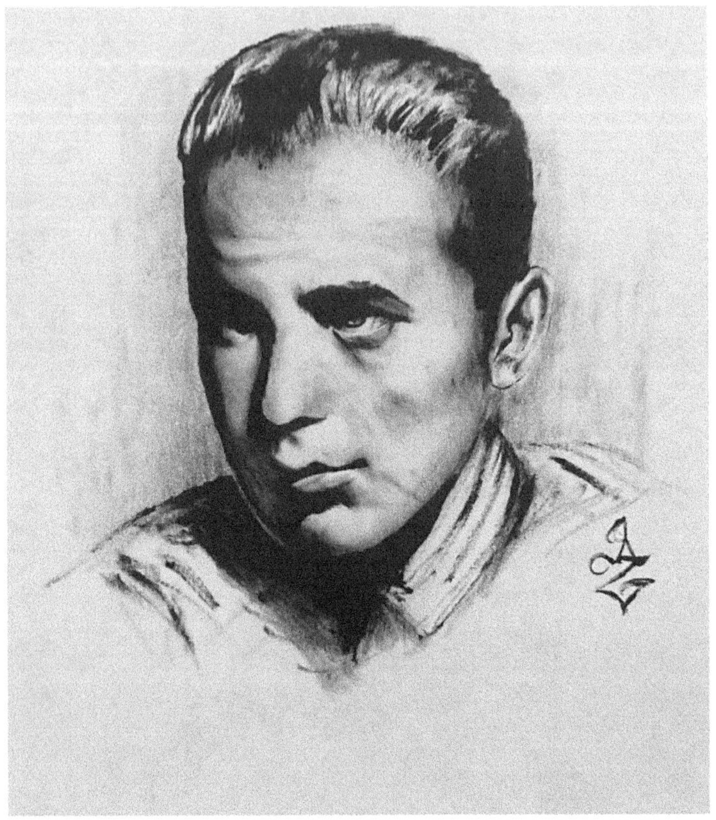

Figure 5.8 Young Humphrey, by Chad Merrill, courtesy of the artist.

> I spent almost every waking minute painting and trying to find my rhythm. I had never painted or drawn anything before that. I can't tell you how I obsessed about painting. I wouldn't want to sleep b/c I needed to paint. It gave me this real outlet I never had, excuse me, I've had outlets in the past but was too dumb to recognize them. What used to take me 14–16 hours to do I can now do in 2–3. I still use the same materials but am currently out of card stock and have been using the inside of little Debbie Cake boxes bought on canteen. I'm working on getting more paper but we can't buy it at my custody level so it's going to be a while before I can buy some of my own . . ..

But that's how much it means to me to paint. It has literally changed my life. I'm not saying I'm some saint or anything like that, what I'm saying is that I can see the sun and these little bits of positivity that weren't visible before and I'm slowly making these productive changes using art. I'm far from perfect, Mr. Whitman and honestly a little nervous about exposing my truth to you like this b/c I think that if you knew what an asshole I used to be before seeing my art you probably wouldn't have given it a second look and now that you know a little bit about me you may still change your mind and that's ok. It's your choice but at least let me say Thank you for validating what I've spent so much of my time, pouring my heart into and ultimately live doing. It means a great deal to me that my art is free even if I'm not.

David Neff has posted an interview with Merrill here: https://prisonjournalismproject.org/2024/01/07/how-one-artist-paints-in-prison/. Merrill's website is: www.chadmerrillart.com/. Additional artwork is posted on the JAC website: https://thejusticeartscoalition.org/portfolio/chad-merrill/.

Robert A. Odom, North Carolina

As a self-taught artist, Robert Odom specializes in graphite and charcoal, producing mostly portraits. In his own words:

I was a biracial kid born in Lansdale, Pennsylvania on May 21st, 1981. My father was a black man from Memphis, Tennessee and my mother is a white woman from Budapest, Hungary. I am a "military brat" and I was raised in places like Landsdale, Germany, and Missouri until we settled in Fayetteville, North Carolina where my father was stationed at Fort Bragg. With my father in the military and my mother working as a secretary almost everywhere she was employed, we weren't rich but we weren't poor either. Around the time I was 10 years old, I can remember the physical, emotional, social, and verbal abuse really starting to gain steam by BOTH parents. But the relationship with my little brother, Joey, and I had with our parents was not the only one suffering. The relationship between themselves didn't survive and they were divorced after my mother walked out on us and left us in that environment – a fact that I don't know, still, if I'll ever forgive her for.

I learned how to draw through relentless practice and trial and error over the last decade. It also helped that I was in the presence of some great artists over the years. I was able to pick their brains and learn some of their tricks of the trade. Others in here write books, screenplays, songs and poetry. I've seen guys build life-size (to scale) dirtbikes using

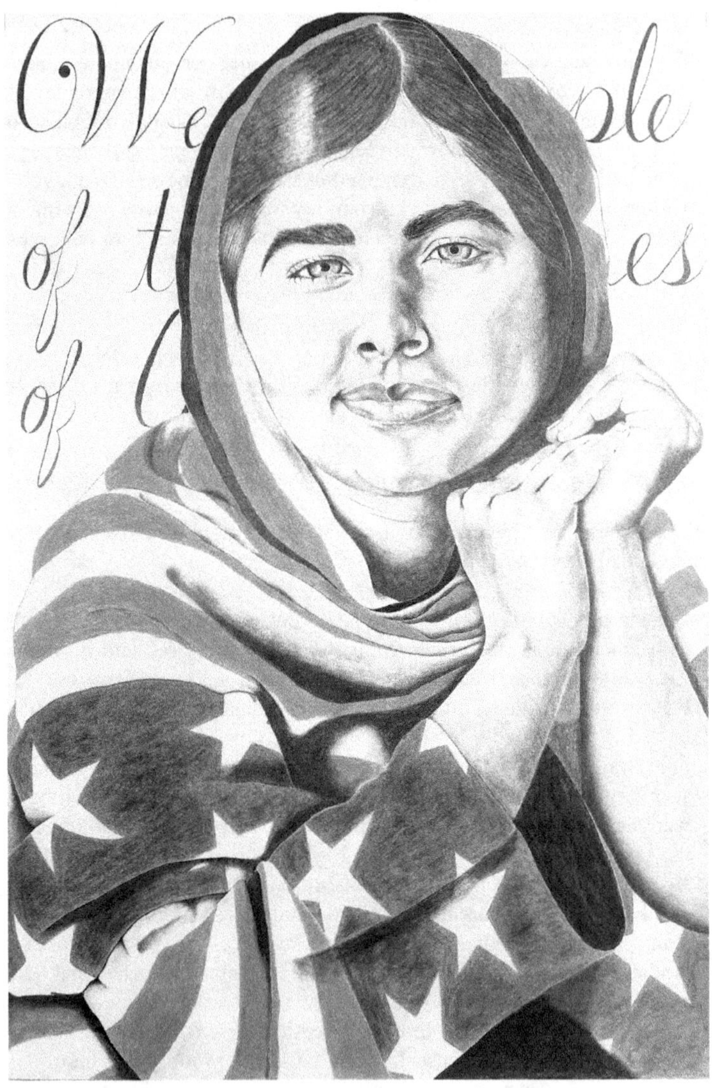

Figure 5.9 American Muslimah, by Robert A. Odom, courtesy of the artist.

> whatever they can find in the trash! Of course it's not operational but the finished product was amazing! The literary work is really awesome as well. One guy I know had his book turned into a movie! We watched it at prison here.
>
> Getting guys access to social media platforms to showcase their talents/creativity is definitely needed. I think the Justice Arts Coalition serves as an awesome example of how to achieve this. Well, my art is a step in the right direction towards financial security as a convicted felon. I can work for myself and save money by working from home. Plus, the artwork can be seen on a wider scale which means people can get access to the story behind the art as well.

I asked if there was anything else to share about his creativity in detention: "Only that we need all the help we can get as artists in a carceral setting."

Odom's work can be seen at:

Instagram: @robertsprisonblues
Facebook: "Robert's Prison Blues"

Victoria Scott, Maine

Victoria writes that she has always been an avid reader and began engaging in theater through church and school, but had a negative experience with a teacher that made her withdraw. She engaged in writing with the support of an education coordinator and advocate for engaging women in the arts. In her own words:

> I cannot describe the feeling that overtakes me when I am working on a story or screenplay. It's like watching a premier by yourself in an IMAX theater. I release my inhibitions, self-criticism, preconceived notions, and allow myself to channel a journey that belongs perhaps to someone else, but feels intimate in its evocative nature. As I write, I myself am surprised by what happens next and despite the fact that I'm the "writer" I feel a bit more like a witness who is learning about the intricacies of the human condition.
>
> Creativity is a stabilizing gravity that decompresses the weight of life's trauma. Creativity isn't simply a practice, but a language that we use to share our emotions that is immediately recognized by the humanity in others.

Victoria Scott shares a memorable account reproduced, with permission, in the box.

Box 5.2 Why I Never Look Over My Shoulder (Run for Your Life), by Victoria Scott

I'm ashamed of my past. I've come a long way and I'm proud of the woman I've become following every moment leading up to right now, but I still feel bashful and protective of my haunted history. I've become a rather good magician, transforming one thing to another, working a little sleight of hand, concealing what would ruin the trick, and being a hell of a showman about it. This is not to say that I consider myself a facade or that my manifestations are not the genuine article, but that I tend to obscure the parts of my life that have hurt me the most. The alchemy is real, but the materials are raw and secret.

Minimizing is how I cope . . .. Where I come from, showing someone the chinks in your armor, your greatest insecurity, an old wound that still is tender under pressure, is an invitation for weaponized exploitation. No matter how resilient I've become, my body still remembers how that feels. I know I'm not that girl anymore . . . but sometimes I still feel her in my skin.

It's a strange thing. I'd almost rather anyone read what they splashed across the front page about me than have them know the truth. I'd rather they know what I did, *or what they think I did*, than confess to them what other people have done *to* me. Secret keeping. It's what I do best. My mother should have named me Irony. I don't keep my own secrets though. I've told anyone who's ever asked why I'm in prison, whether they were a fly-by-night quad-mate or the alumni gathering at MIT. The harder words to choke out were where I'm from, who I've met, and how I let myself be treated. Each disclosure stung like a canker on the tip of my tongue. Maybe if I let everyone think I'm a monster it will make me feel safer. If they think I'm dangerous maybe they won't try to injure me. If they *know* I'm broken, they may test my fractures with rough hands and harder hearts, harsh words and acts cruel and unusual. They have before.

When the police arrived, I trauma-vomited all over the detective who took an interest in me; he promised to keep me safe and held my hand when they stitched up the knife wound in my thigh at the hospital. I'd met the cop before that night, when he responded to an incident at my house involving my sister, I was just 14 then. Now I was 10 years older and none-the-wiser. That night I unburdened myself and told him more than I meant to about who'd been hurting me lately and how, the things that happened in someone's cousin's basement bedroom or in wooded driveways at night.

After I was arrested, I had a dream that the State Troopers and State's Attorneys came to my funeral and laughed in front of my casket while the pastor gave a eulogy. My nightmare came to life during my trial as I listened to the detective, the same man that had held my hand in the hospital, tell the jury that I was a weirdo; a cold, calculated liar; and he compared holding my hand to cradling a woman's dead child. "Sometimes you have to do things in the line of duty you really don't want to do."

The 911 calls, assault reports and PFA petitions I've filed, polite inquiries, requests for assistance, and explanations make me feel small, helpless. What's worse are the stories I don't tell, the incidents I'm unwilling to explain. Maybe I don't keep these secrets for me. Maybe I keep them because I know that no one really cares. All I know is, it's in the past . . . and I'm not going back there.

Cuong Mike Tran, California

Cuong Mike Tran was born in 1980 to parents who fled Vietnam in 1975 and arrived in Altoona, Pennsylvania, where he entered the world. He writes:

> My family grew up in poverty, but we fought hard to appear otherwise. We were often victims of crime because of the shape of our eyes. I learned early on that my very existence could inspire hate and violence. I eventually turned that hate inward, only to turn it back on the world. I remember my dad making prop battleships out of cardboard, because we could not afford to buy toys. At a young age I would create my own toys out of paper and cardboard for the same reasons. I found out early on that I had a natural ability to draw and create. I am self-taught in prison. My passion for art was rediscovered and reignited in here. Don't forget the humans in here. Look at our art and seek to understand us. Don't ask, "What's wrong." Instead ask, "What happened." Hear our voices and our stories through our art.

As is often the case, an incarcerated artist like Tran is limited for inspiration and practice to works published in books and magazines protected by copyright, restricting the material that can be reproduced without permission. Here, Tran copies Vermeer's *The Milkmaid* (1658) on flattened cardboard, imaginatively framing the image of a masterpiece inside the busted-open sides of a prison lunchbox, invoking a metaphorical release of creativity from prison.

More of Tran's work can be seen here: https://thejusticeartscoalition.org/portfolio/cuong-mike-tran/

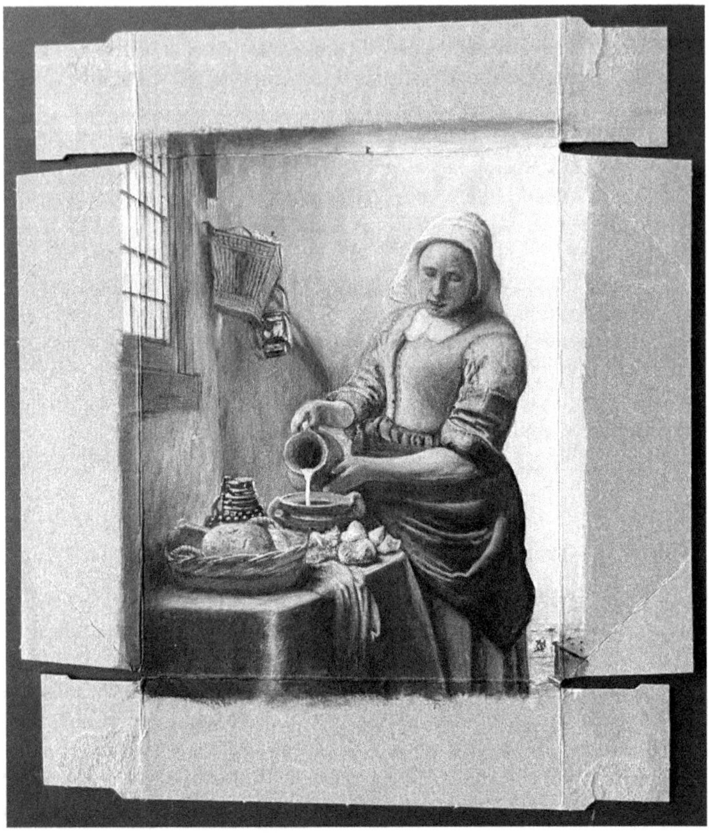

Figure 5.10 *Vermeer's maidservant pouring milk*, by Cuong Mike Tran, courtesy of the artist.

Robert Lee Williams, New York

Robert Lee Williams, born in Poughkeepsie, New York, to a woman with PCP addiction in 1983, was adopted and raised by a cousin and never met his alcoholic father. From an early age, he began performing, rapping, and competing with other boys. He dropped out of 11th grade to start "running the streets, rapping" and later formed a performing group called Generation Threat. He started learning about music production, but his life took a turn when he joined the Bloods at 19.

In prison, Williams studied writing with John J. Lennon, the acclaimed prison journalist, and now receives compensation for his published works, which have appeared in Lithub, PEN America, PJP, and *Plough Quarterly*. Williams notes,

> John's publicist told me a story about when a conservative journalist read my "Prison Parenting piece it changed how she thought about her daughters' phone usage. I read a comment that it made a 70-year-old man cry. Our stories matter. Our creativity is how we express it.

Other Visual Arts Examples

While the following artists, some recently discharged from incarceration, were not included in my study, I selected examples of their work to provide further evidence of contemporary creativity in prison. All works are reproduced with permission from the creators. Links are provided for biographical information and additional art.

AEmilius 7, Texas

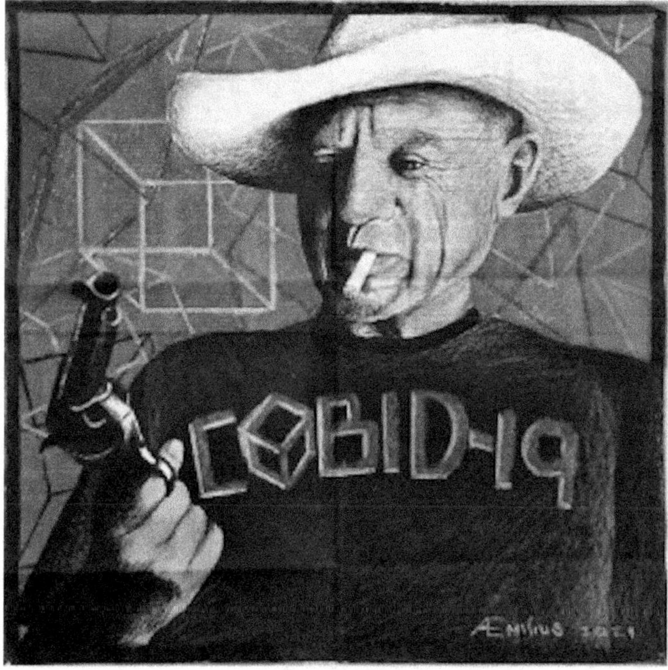

Figure 5.11 Le Peintre De La Vie Moderne, by AEmilius 7, courtesy of the artist.

Mark Andreason, location unknown

For additional works, see https://thejusticeartscoalition.org/portfolio/mark-andreason/.

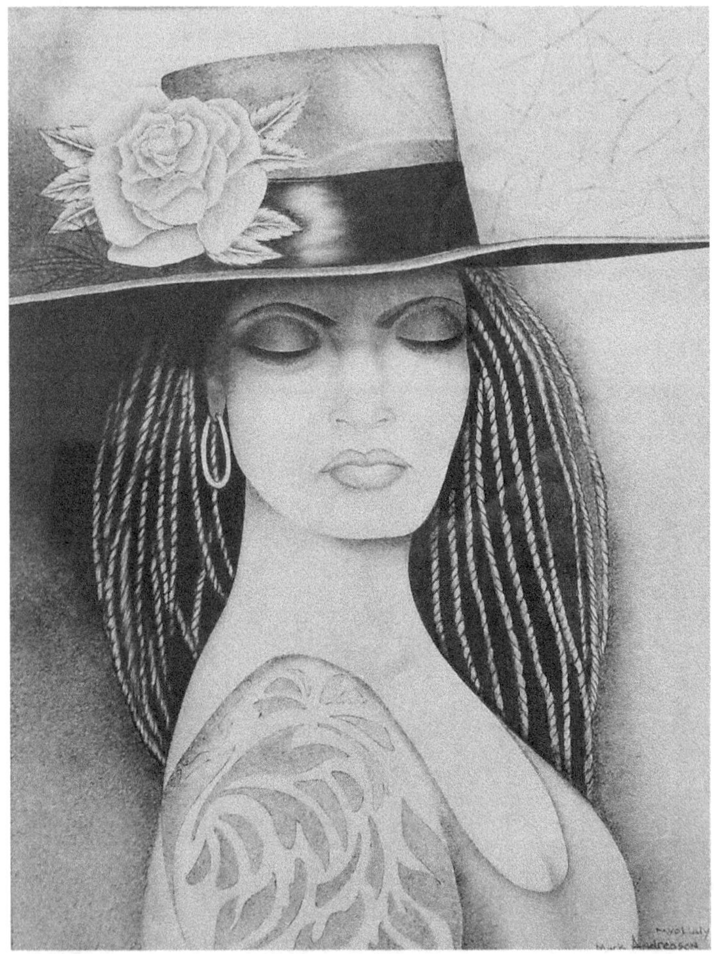

Figure 5.12 My Ol' lady, by Mark Andreason, courtesy of the artist.

Anthony Graff, Iowa

For additional works, see https://thejusticeartscoalition.org/portfolio/tony-graff/.

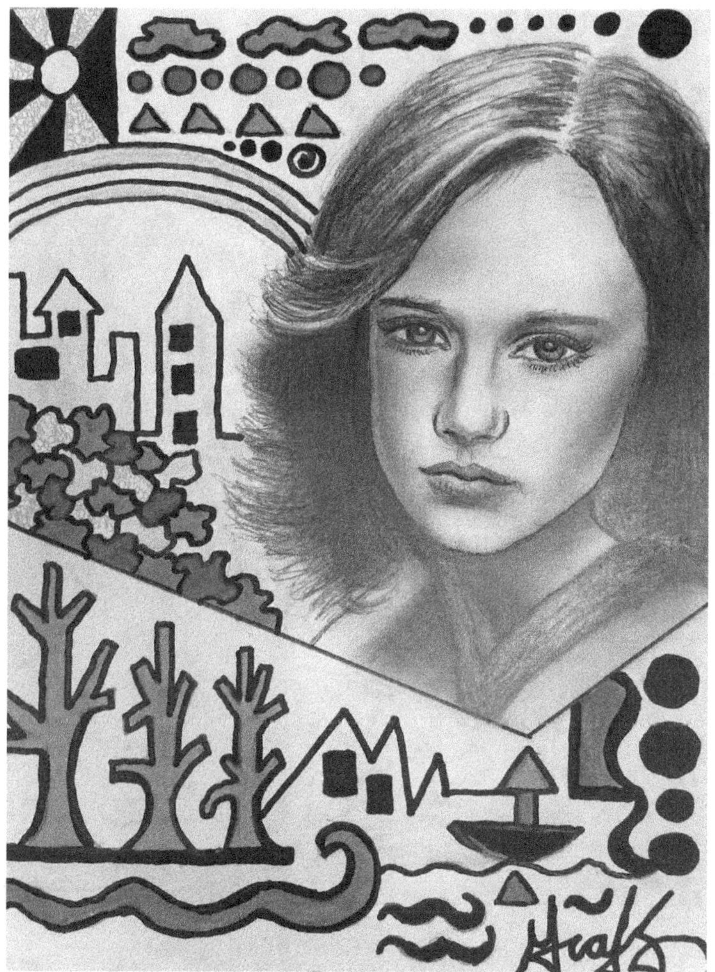

Figure 5.13 Forever, by Tony Graff, courtesy of the artist.

Bednago Harper, Illinois

For additional works, see https://thejusticeartscoalition.org/portfolio/bednago-harper/.

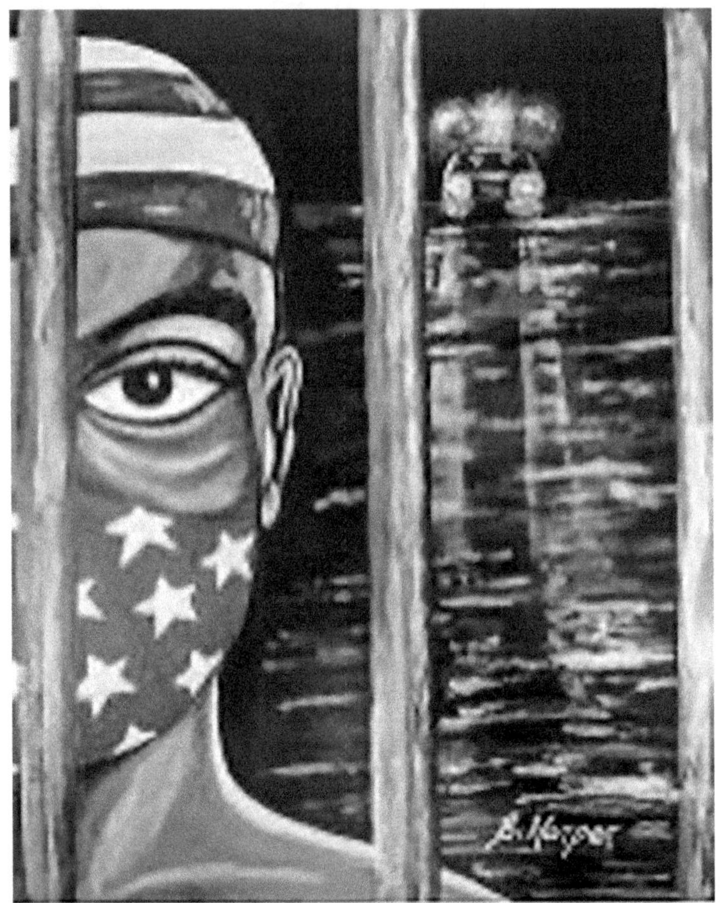

Figure 5.14 Land of the free, by Bednago Harper, courtesy of the artist.

kidwifdacrayons, Maryland

For additional works, see https://thejusticeartscoalition.org/portfolio/kid-wif-da-crayons-kw-dc/

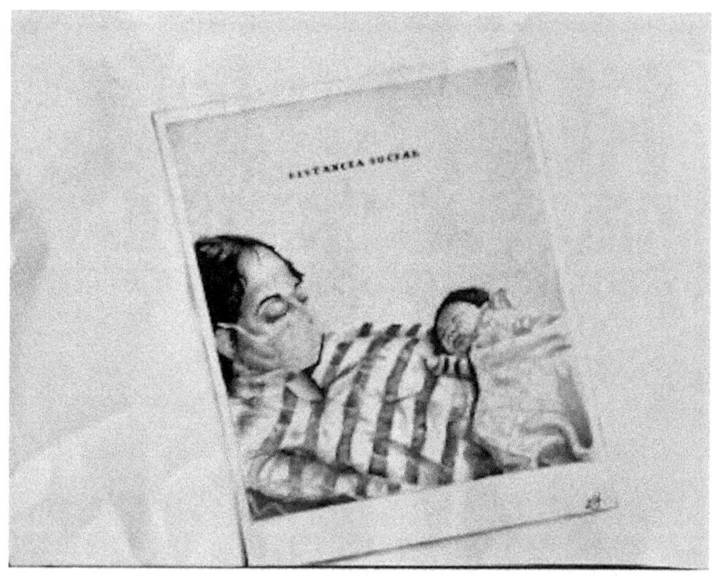

Figure 5.15 Distancia social, by kidwifdacrayons, courtesy of the artist.

William B. Livingston, III, Oklahoma

For additional works, see https://thejusticeartscoalition.org/portfolio/william-b-livingston-iii/.

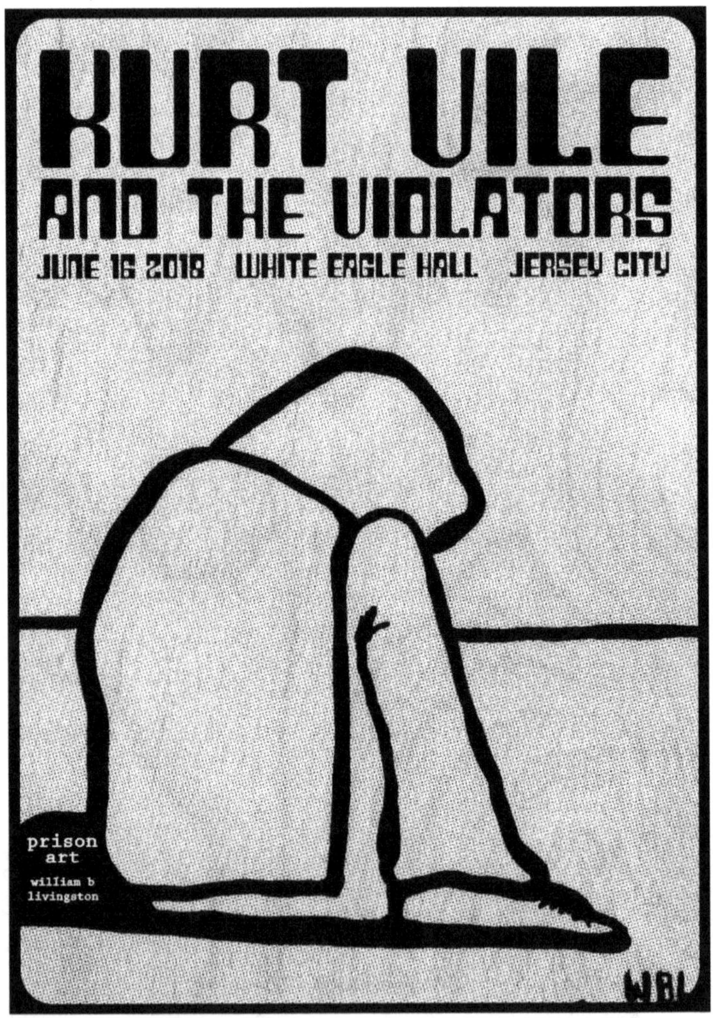

Figure 5.16 Kurt Vile poster, by William B. Livingston, III, courtesy of the artist.

FREER Records Recording Artists

FREER Records, formerly Die Jim Crow, is a nonprofit recording studio assisting people in prison to record and sell their musical creations. Founder Fury Young offers the following collection produced at FREER as a sample of musical creations prepared by prison musicians. Notes are drawn from descriptions provided by FREER Records. All links and notes are published with permission by FREER Records. If you are not able to activate these links, these artists can be found through the FREER website, www.freerrecords.com/.

Michael Austin, Maryland

In 1974, Mike Austin was sentenced to prison for a crime he did not commit. During 27 years in prison, music was his sanctuary. He was exonerated in 2001 and received financial restitution for his wrongful conviction.

Is It Hope [song], with Lifers Groove, recorded on Groove Therapy [album]

Carl Dukes, New York

Plastic Bag was composed by Carl Dukes and Ben Pagano. Dukes spent over 30 years in New York State prisons and was released to become homeless for three months, an experience described in his story. Apostle Heloise, who was in New York State prisons for four years, joins vocals with Dukes.

Plastic Bag [song], recorded on Die Jim Crow E.P. [album]
Riverflow [song], with Lifers Groove, recorded on Groove Therapy [album]

Cedric Johnson, Kansas

On completion of a multi-year sentence at the Kansas Lansing Correctional Facility, Cedric Johnson conceived I'm Home in a motel room and recorded the first official release with Die Jim Crow, now FREER Records. I'm Home was released on 1 March 2015.

I'm Home [song], recorded on Die Jim Crow E.P. [album]

Anthony McKinney, Ohio

Tired & Weary was written by Anthony "Big Ant" McKinney about a crime he denies committing. Incarcerated in 2005, McKinney sings vocals on this recording made at Warren Correctional Institution, Lebanon, Ohio.

Tired & Weary [song], recorded on Die Jim Crow E.P. [album]

Maxwell Melvins, New Jersey

Melvins, released on parole in 2011, had by then served 33 years of a life sentence in New Jersey. In prison, he started the Grammy-nominated hip-hop Lifers Group. Struggling with mental and physical health, he aims to help reduce barriers to creativity in prison and change how Black men are represented in the arts and media.

Drapetomania [song], with Lifers Groove, recorded on Groove Therapy [album]

Dane Newton, Colorado

Dane Newton, a.k.a. Zealot, entered the world in 1981 surrounded by gangs and violence in South Bakersfield, California, where he was recruited to join a gang at 13. He escaped to Denver, Colorado, in 2006 only to re-engage in the old ways, which landed him in prison and sentenced to 36 years.

Battlecry '14 [song], with Territorial, recorded on Tlaxihuiqui [album]
America the Merciful [song], with Territorial, recorded on Tlaxihuiqui [album]

Mark B. Springer, Ohio

A215–162 is the prison number belonging to Mark B. Springer, who wrote the lyrics with Sedrick Franklin. Springer has been incarcerated since 1989, serving time in various prisons. The men's choir is composed of residents at the Warren Correctional Institution. The women's choir consists of formerly incarcerated women, recorded in Brooklyn, New York.

My Name Be Jim Crow [song], recorded on Die Jim Crow E.P. [album]

Naomi Blount Wilson, Pennsylvania

Simply Naomi grew up in North Philadelphia under the spell of her mother's gospel voice. She learned to sing and play piano at 8, and by her teenage years was recorded by Swan Records. In 1982, Wilson was sentenced to life at Muncy State Prison, where she led the Lady Lifers choir. After 37 years, her sentence was commuted in 2019.

Mello-D [song], with Lifers Groove, recorded on Groove Therapy [album]

Kevin Woodley, Colorado

Kevin Woodley was born and grew up in Chicago. He had been incarcerated for over two decades prior to his release in 2023. He continues to sing despite severe health conditions requiring an oxygen tank.

My Name Ain't Jim Crow [song], with Territorial, recorded on Tlaxihuiqui [album]

Bonus Track

This track features several artists who have recorded with FREER Records: Maxwell Melvins, Simply Naomi, Michael Austin, Valerie Seeley, Carl Dukes, and Brian Lawlor.

Driftin' [song], with Lifers Groove, recorded on Groove Therapy [album]

▪ ▪ ▪

In economic terms, creators in prison would represent the *supply side* of a prison creativity enterprise. But, as incarcerated artists like those we have met in the past few pages know too well, it is virtually impossible to be creative without support. All the accoutrements required for creativity – paper, pencils, brushes, paints, instruments for musicians – that are otherwise taken for granted are difficult to obtain in many prisons that do not have a HobbyCraft program. Creators are largely dependent on assistance from the outside for the materials they need. Some are self-taught, others are tutored by fellow residents, and many benefit from arts-in-corrections teachers from the outside to learn artistic skills. Let's meet some of the leading organizations engaged in supporting incarcerated creators and facilitating their work.

Notes

1 See: https://ias.ucsc.edu/visualizing-abolition/exhibitions/ and https://ias.ucsc.edu/exhibitions-events/exhibitions/, cited 29 April 2024.
2 Annenkovna was discharged in July 2024.
3 See: www.jaiquanfayson.com/drawing-freedom, cited 8 February 2024.
4 LaMarr Knox's work can be seen by searching for Knox at www.themarshallproject.org, cited 31 July 2024.
5 See: www.imdb.com/media/rm3594754048/nm0000007, cited 10 February 2024.

References

Bell, R. Z. (2020). *Tales of Vrenarri: Red summer*. Self Published.

Kilgannon, C. (2024, February 18). How a notorious jail became a literary hotbed. *The New York Times*. www.nytimes.com/2024/02/18/nyregion/rikers-island-authors.html cited 18 February 2024.

Lennon, J. J. (2019, October 28). The apology letter. *The Washington Post*. www.washingtonpost.com/magazine/2019/10/28/ive-built-career-prolific-prison-journalist-so-why-did-it-take-me-so-long-write-letter-family-man-i-killed/?arc404=true cited 28 October 2019.

Merts, P. (2022). *Ex crucible: The passion of incarcerated artists*. Daylight Community Arts Foundation and Daylight Books.

Whitman, J. R. (2024). Intellectual property empowerment and protection for prisoners. In S. Jamar & L. Mtima (Eds.), *Handbook of intellectual property and social justice* (pp. 245–264). Cambridge University Press. https://doi.org/10.1017/9781108697613

6 Leading Facilitators

The prospect of introducing new, creative products emerging from carceral facilities raises the question of how they can best enter the supply chain to reach potential customers in a market for such goods. At the origin of the creative enterprise are individual creators working alone or in groups, such as through arts-in-corrections programs. Once expressive works are produced with the intention of distribution, they should be protected by copyright registration. Then they must be made available to prospective intermediaries, such as publishers or art galleries, to become available to end users. While I have characterized the prison population as being equivalent to the fifth largest city, *Prisonopolis*, that metaphor belies the fact that individual creators are spread across the nation in different facilities, creating a greater supply chain challenge to locate, collect, and disseminate their works.

Thankfully, a number of individuals and nonprofit organizations are already engaged as disconnected links of such a supply chain. These pioneers are facilitating creativity in detention. I introduce several of them here in order to demonstrate that elements of a supply chain exist and thus provide evidence of both creativity at work in prisons and also the potential of an incipient supply chain infrastructure. I will describe such an infrastructure, a proposed Nationwide Carceral Creativity Framework, in the following chapter.

First, I must recognize and salute the many teachers who, as employees, contractors, or volunteers, are committed to helping the incarcerated enrich their lives through learning. As one prison reformer points out, it's not a program that makes a difference in someone's life; it's another person (Keller, 2022, p. 142). Such educators are truly an unsung national treasure. Another category of valuable contributors includes non-governmental organizations that provide information, advocacy, and monitoring services to increase understanding of the overall justice system in the United States. Such organizations include the Justice Policy Center of the Urban Institute, the Marshall Project, the Prison Policy Initiative, the Vera Institute of Justice, the Women's Prison Association, and around the world, organizations such as the European Society of Criminology, Penal Reform International, and the World Prison Brief (see Appendix A: Resources).

DOI: 10.4324/9781003566021-7

In addition, a number of entities currently provide a wide range of services directly in support of arts-in-corrections. Information on many such programs can be found in the Americans for the Arts website that provides a searchable database of national arts publications,[1] as well as in the *Art for Justice Fund Directory* and website.[2] Grady Hillman provides the names and organizations of arts-in-corrections expertise in the Southwest in his book, *Arts in Corrections* (Hillman, 2023), and he, Amanda Gardner, and Lori Hager offer an online annotated bibliography of prison arts resources, "Prison Arts Resource Project: An Annotated Bibliography," updated in April 2018 (Gardner et al., 2014). In addition, the JAC maintains an online database of writing and arts programs.[3]

In this section, I include exemplary programs to convey the diversity and engagement of people and organizations with an intentional effort to support the arts in prison. For more complete coverage, consult the above sources and publications that document the work of such efforts in detail. For example, in *Paths of Discovery: Art and Practice and Its Impact in California Prisons*, second edition, the authors Larry Brewster and Peter Merts, recount the arts-in-corrections experience in California, beginning with Governor Jerry Brown's initiative in the 1970s to explore how to engage the arts in state institutions, including prisons. This led to the establishment of the Prison Arts Project, with support from the William James Association (WJA), followed by legislation in 1980 to establish the Arts-in-Corrections program in California.

The California art in corrections program continued for nearly 30 years until 2003, when government support was largely shut down due to a state budget crisis, only to be resurrected beginning in 2014 without California civil service employee engagement of arts facilitators who had previously coordinated the programs at each prison. *Paths of Discovery* notes the participation of some 19 different organizations but focuses in detail on the work of the WJA, the Marin Shakespeare Company, The Actors' Gang, and Jail Guitar Doors (JGD), representing the range of arts under the rubric of "fine arts" programs. The book is fortified with testimonials from residents attesting to the value of their experiences as participants. The authors write that whatever their paths to prison, residents are motivated to tell stories that the public needs to hear (Brewster & Merts, 2015, p. 140).

Below are brief notes on selected intermediary and service organizations and, in some cases, the people who founded or led them. I know several of these leaders and can say that there is not an exploitative bone in any of them. They are truly devoted advocates for people in prison, which is why they choose to work through nonprofit organizations. However, some smaller organizations may face leadership and funding challenges. Some have already closed but are included to acknowledge the significance of their contribution.

Each organizational profile ends with an indication of its functional capability category: "Production" (engaged in training and/or supporting residents to develop their creative skills); "Library" (engaged in providing residents with access to inspirational books and materials as well as research assistance); "Intermediation" (providing services for publishing or recording creative works for distribution); and "Logistics" (providing advocacy and assistance for intellectual property registration, educational technology, program funding, fee assistance, banking services, and access to other types of service providers).

Alabama Prison Arts and Education Project

The Alabama Prison Arts and Education Project (APAEP) was founded and is directed by Kyes Stevens at Auburn University. APAEP provides arts and educational engagement to people who are incarcerated or formerly incarcerated in Alabama.[4] Programs include printmaking classes, mural projects, a traveling exhibit of art, student anthology, drawing instruction, and a concert series at state prisons. Students have published 16 anthologies of their literature and hosted 11 exhibits of their artwork. Of some 43,000 people in detention in the state,[5] 6,500 students have been served to date, indicating a need that far exceeds available resources.

Stevens conceived of the project in 2001 when she was teaching poetry with a Fellowship from the National Endowment for the Arts (NEA) at the Talladega Federal Prison. She first received funding for the project from the NEA in 2003. Stevens is a poet and historian whose work, in addition to founding APAEP, includes studying the photographs of the rural South during the Great Depression and documentary materials from the 1930s featuring Gee's Bend, Alabama, perhaps best known for artistic quilts.

Functional category: Production (literature) and Intermediation

American Prison Writing Archive

The leading and largest repository for prison writing is the APWA, founded by educator Doran Larson. According to its website,[6] APWA collects first-person accounts from people living in confinement. Nearly 4,000 essays provide testimony to the actual conditions inside as well as other topics. Unedited essays are digitized and disseminated through the APWA website, which is free and open to the public, scholars, journalists, and policymakers.

Larson is Edward North Professor of Literature at Hamilton College. He led a writing workshop inside Attica Correctional Facility for ten years and organized two college programs inside New York State prisons. He is the author of *Witness in the Era of Mass Incarceration* (2017) and editor of *Fourth City: Essays from the Prison in America* (Larson, 2013). His recent book *Inside Knowledge: Incarcerated People on the Failures of the American Prison* was published by NYU Press (Larson, 2024). I had the pleasure of reviewing his book in the *Howard Journal of Crime and Justice* (Whitman, 2024a).

APWA is an outgrowth of Larson's book, *Fourth City*. Funding from the National Endowment for the Humanities sustained the project from 2017 to 2021 and a grant from The Mellon Foundation in 2022 enabled expansion, wider dissemination, and relocation of the APWA to the Sheridan Libraries at Johns Hopkins University. According to *Inside Knowledge*, APWA will be succeeded by the Prison Witness Collective, which will expand the scope of submissions to include essays from others in the justice system and to assist writers in placing their works for publication in books and journals.

Functional category: Production (literature) and Intermediation

Art for Justice Fund

The Art for Justice Fund (A4J) stands out for its leadership and its impact on facilitating arts in prisons.[7] Founded by philanthropist Agnes Gund in 2017, A4J catalyzed a variety of social justice initiatives to end mass incarceration, including supporting more than 200 artists and advocacy organizations. By the time A4J ended in 2023, some $127 million had been invested, including amounts contributed by the Ford Foundation and Rockefeller Philanthropy Advisors. Three inspirational works shaped Gund's views on the injustice of mass incarceration and compelled her to establish the fund: Michelle Alexander's book, *The New Jim Crow* (Alexander, 2010/2012), Bryan Stevenson's book, *Just Mercy*, (Stevenson, 2014), and Ava DuVernay's powerful documentary, *13th*, which explains how Blacks were systematically imprisoned after being freed from slavery (Du Vernay, 2016).

The A4J website continues to offer resources, including the *Art for Justice Fund Directory* of individuals and organizations supported by the Fund between 2017 and 2023.[8]

Functional category: Logistics

California Lawyers for the Arts

Founded in 1974, California Lawyers for the Arts (CLA) provides legal services to members of the creative arts community, including access to legal assistance, dispute resolution, education, and advocacy.[9] Since 2011, CLA has been a pioneer in the movement to promote creativity in prisons, collaborating with Dr. Larry Brewster, emeritus professor of public administration at the University of San Francisco, to design evidence-based research that showed the value of arts programs in the state prison system. CLA began its national arts-in-corrections expansion project in 2015 with a series of conferences and forums that resulted in demonstration projects in Louisiana, Texas, and New York. CLA also initiated Designing Creative Futures, providing paid four-month internships for formerly incarcerated people seeking careers in the arts. CLA places returning residents released within the past seven years in arts organizations based on their mutual interests. More than 140 interns have received career and educational counseling in addition to hands-on training from experienced artists and administrators.

To quote from Brewster's book (Brewster & Merts, 2015, p. 13),

> Many have advocated for and worked on behalf of California prison fine arts programs, but no one has done so harder and smarter than Alma Robinson, Executive Director of California Lawyers for the Arts . . .. She is a talented, tenacious, and endearing advocate for the arts who led the charge to re-fund prison arts programs alongside veterans Laurie Brooks, Jack Bowers, Lesley Currier, Sabra Williams, Tim Robbins, and Wayne Kramer.

Robinson, a graduate of Middlebury College and Stanford Law School, has served on national committees including the Free at Last Coalition and Abolish Slavery National Network, working to correct the 13th Amendment to the U.S. Constitution. She is a former journalist, founding board member of California Arts Advocates and the Museum of the African Diaspora, and former trustee of the San Francisco Opera Association and Mills College.[10]

Functional category: Logistics

Copyright Alliance

The Copyright Alliance (CA) was founded in 2007 as a nonprofit, social welfare organization advocating for policies to bolster the value of copyright and the interests of creators who produce expressive works that qualify for copyright protection as well as corporations such as publishers and movie producers that market and sell creative works.[11] As a social welfare organization, CA is permitted to engage in political lobbying and campaign efforts to support or oppose specific policies, bonds, and referendums, and thus contributions are not tax deductible.

CA has both institutional and individual members.[12] Its over 60-member trade organizations include those among the most recognizable names in the entertainment industry, representing millions of creative workers. CA also represents over 23,000 individual creators – writers, composers, recording artists, journalists, filmmakers, visual artists, photographers, software developers, and many others.

The CA website offers numerous educational resources to learn about copyright as well as a directory of copyright attorneys. Its programs include Community Partnerships, open at no cost to all organizations that share the mission to protect creators, and the Initiative to Promote Diversity in Copyright, which supports Black creators, Indigenous creators, and other creators of color to engage in the copyright system, including filing registrations at no cost to the creator.

Functional category: Logistics

Ear Hustle

In a novel genre, Ear Hustle is a podcast specifically created to develop content mostly by and for incarcerated people.[13] This venture began in 2017 as the first of its kind, a podcast created and produced behind bars at the San Quentin State Prison in California. The show was co-founded by Nigel Poor, an artist in the Bay Area, and Earlonne Woods and Antwan Williams, who were incarcerated at the time of inception.

Nigel Poor and Earlonne Woods continue to produce the award-winning show. Poor began her engagement by volunteering to teach through the Mount Tamalpais College, previously known as the Prison University Project. As a visual artist, her work has appeared nationally and internationally. She is a professor of photography at California State University in Sacramento and with Nigel Poor has coauthored *This Is Ear Hustle: Unflinching Stories of Everyday Prison Life* (Crown Publishing Group, 2022).

Earlonne Woods, originally from Los Angeles, received a 31-year sentence. In prison, he completed his GED, took courses with Coastline Community College, and completed vocational training programs. He founded an effort to repeal California's Three Strikes Law, called CHOOSE1, and cofounded Ear Hustle. After 21 years inside, his sentence was commuted by California's governor and he then joined PRX as a producer.

Functional category: Production (Other) and Intermediation

First Step Alliance

First Step Alliance (FSA) was founded in 2021 as a nonprofit organization established to facilitate successful community reentry after incarceration and to assist returning citizens achieve financial independence through access to banking services and financial education.[14] FSA has begun the process to establish a Federal Credit Union for incarcerated and formerly incarcerated individuals and their families, a much-needed capacity to address the needs of the currently unbanked in this population throughout the country. Estimates of the unbanked in the justice system range from 1.4% of adults in the population (Watson, 2019) to 29% of incarcerated adults (Kaushal et al., 2021).

Nancy Eiden, FSA founder, board chair, and secretary, has worked in wealth management, marketing, operations, and regulatory compliance at global banks and credit unions for three decades. She holds a number of securities industry licenses and is a Certified Mentor with SCORE, serves on the board of the Center for LGBTQ Economic Advancement and Research, as an Ambassador for New Jersey Reentry Corporation, and Advisory Council Member with

Farm Sahel, a nonprofit concerned with gender equity and food security in West Africa. Nancy received her BS in Economics from the Wharton School.

Functional category: Logistics

FREER Records

FREER Records (formerly Die Jim Crow) offers recording and distribution services for prison residents.[15] FREER was founded in 2013 by Fury Young, who serves as Co-Executive Director with BL Shirelle, a formerly incarcerated musician and educator. In 2013, Young was inspired by Occupy Wall Street and the personal experiences of his close friend, Alexander Pridgen,[16] a Black Muslim who had been Muhammed Ali's bodyguard and served time.

Fury began reading Michelle Alexander's *The New Jim Crow* while listening to Pink Floyd's *The Wall*, inspiring him to make a concept album about racial injustice in the prison system. Under Young's leadership, FREER has gained access to five prisons and recorded full bands, choirs, and solo musicians, totaling over 60 incarcerated artists and over a dozen formerly incarcerated artists. Young's first full-length album for FREER as producer/art director was Territorial's *Tlaxihuiqui*.

According to its website, FREER Records is the first record label in the United States for musicians affected by prison. Its aim is to replace stereotypes by amplifying the voices of musician artists, including musicians in the Black, LGBTQIA+, immigrant, indigenous, women, poor white, and otherwise marginalized communities.

Functional category: Production (music) and Intermediation

Institute for Intellectual Property and Social Justice

A key theme in this book is the importance of protecting intellectual property for all creators, including those in incarceration. The Institute for Intellectual Property and Social Justice (IIPSJ) is a champion for protecting IP among marginalized groups.[17] According to its website, the mission of IIPSJ is to pursue the social justice obligations of intellectual property protection by promoting core principles of access, inclusion, and empowerment. IIPSJ principals, scholars, and practitioners examine IP law and policy to identify areas where full participation by underrepresented groups needs redressing. IIPSJ undertakes a variety of programs and activities, including IIPSJ CLE (continuing legal education), an annual, international conference on IP and social justice, and IP MOSAIC, an annual convening of academics, policy leaders, and activists to critique IP protection.

IIPSJ is an accredited Non-governmental Organization Member of the World Intellectual Property Organization (WIPO). Lateef Mtima founded and co-directs IIPSJ with Steven Jamar. Mtima is professor of law at the Howard

University School of Law. After graduating with honors from Amherst College, Professor Mtima received his JD degree from Harvard Law School, where he was the cofounder and later editor-in-chief of the *Harvard Black Letter Journal*.

Steven Jamar is codirector of IIPSJ and serves as its associate director for scholarly initiatives, responsible for producing the *Cambridge Handbook of Intellectual Property and Social Justice* (Jamar & Mtima, 2024). Jamar is Professor Emeritus of Law at Howard University School of Law, where he taught constitutional law and copyright law. He earned his J.D. from Hamline University School of Law in St. Paul, Minnesota, and his L.L.M. from Georgetown University Law School. His publications include many works on copyright and international human rights.

A small team of advocates, including law professor Viva Moffat, law student Eliza Granger, and lawyer and trademark examiner Robin Oroma Womeodu, have worked with me in collaboration with IIPSJ to prepare a protocol to facilitate registration of copyrights for people in prison. Our presentation at the 2023 MOSAIC conference provides an overview of our respective efforts in this area.[18] To raise attention to this need among the legal community, Professor Moffat has cogently argued in her paper, "The Free Exercise of Copyright Behind Bars" in the *Washington and Lee Law Review*, for taking action to protect copyright registration for people in prison (Moffat, 2023).

Functional category: Logistics

Jail Guitar Doors

Nationwide, a number of organizations are engaged in teaching music in a variety of forms to residents in detention. JGD is a legendary initiative that originated in England in 2007[19] when Billy Bragg founded the organization in honor of his friend Joe Strummer of The Clash, which had a song titled "Jail Guitar Doors" (Bulgren, 2020). In 2009, Wayne Kramer, who did two years in Kentucky's Lexington Federal Prison for dealing cocaine, invited Bragg to conduct a workshop at Sing Sing Correctional Facility in New York, and Kramer started JGD USA later that year.[20]

According to a case study about the organization written by Christopher Bulgren, music instructor at Oregon State University, as of 2020, JGD USA was teaching guitar at 100 facilities, with a waiting list of some 50 others (Bulgren, 2020). The typical arrangement is that JGD USA provides guitars to participating facilities, combined with guitar and song-writing lessons for residents. Bulgren's analysis of participant comments at the Cook County Jail found strong evidence of the productive life skills benefits of engaging in music during incarceration (Bulgren, 2020).

Functional category: Production (music)

Justice Arts Coalition

The JAC described here reflects the organization while under the former leadership of its founder, Wendy Jason. JAC is a nationwide program that promotes the visual and literary arts in corrections.[21] Wendy Jason, who organized JAC in 2019, is a community builder and advocate who combines her background in restorative practices, mental health, and education with her passion for the arts to foster vibrant, inclusive, and nurturing communities that model and promote social justice. She has been in close relationship and/or working in different capacities with currently and formerly incarcerated people for over 25 years.

According to its website, JAC connects current and formerly incarcerated artists with teachers, advocates, and other allies to use the transformative power of art to reimagine justice. JAC conducts a number of programs, including: a correspondence program; a feedback channel to collect public comments on the work of specific artists, art exhibitions, workshops, storytelling through other nonprofits and community organizations; a distance learning program for women in Maryland; and Zoom conferences, volunteering and developing a code of ethics for the prison art community.

Wendy Jason holds a B.A. in Sociology from Eastern Connecticut State University, studied Transformative Language Arts at Goddard College, and completed her M.A. in Coexistence and Conflict through Brandeis University's Alan B. Slifka Program in Intercommunal Coexistence. Her research focused on the intersection of the arts and peacebuilding and culminated in a thesis based on a year spent facilitating creative writing and peace education groups within a county jail. She has taught courses on social justice and conflict transformation in Georgetown University's Program on Justice and Peace, researched and reported on issues related to restorative justice and the arts for Change.org, and has served as the manager of the Prison Arts Coalition website, the predecessor of JAC, for over nine years. She is committed to supporting both individual and social change by cultivating relationships grounded in collaboration, trust, authenticity, empathy, and integrity. I served for several years as an advisor to JAC during Jason's leadership.

Functional category: Production (visual arts and literature) and Intermediation

Library Associations: American Library Association and International Federation of Library Associations and Institutions

The value of libraries to people in prison cannot be overstated. Librarians across the country are working hard to provide such services to people in prison, as attested by prison librarian Jill Grunenwald in her memoir, *Reading*

Behind Bars (Grunenwald, 2019). Robert Lee Williams, writing from the Sullivan Correctional Facility in New York, testifies to the importance of his library, noting the inspiration he received by reading prison journalist John J. Lennon's interview with Reginald Dwayne Betts, who had left prison to become a poet, lawyer, and recipient of a 2021 MacArthur award (Williams, 2023). Arts-in-corrections expert Grady Hillman writes about the rehabilitative intent of prison libraries in the 1950s and 1960s, offering literary growth opportunities in the 1960s and 1970s to personalities including Eldridge Cleaver, Malcolm Braly, Etheridge Knight, Ricardo Sanchez, Raul Salinas, and Michael Hogan (Hillman, 2023, p. 189).

People in prison have a right to reading and other materials available through libraries (Austin, 2022). Prison libraries provide books and materials that can be a source of creative inspiration. Such libraries should be accommodated within carceral institutions and supplemented by public libraries and book services on the outside, making books and other library materials freely available to all people in prison. Such libraries should also highlight works created by other people in prison located anywhere in the prison network and inform residents about the Intellectual Property clause of the Constitution of the United States and how it protects their copyright ownership.

The American Library Association (ALA) offers a resource guide for prison libraries and for reentry.[22] Through the Library Services for the Justice Involved (LSJI) and Office for Diversity, Literacy and Outreach Services (ODLOS), the Association contributes to a listserv hosted by the Colorado State Library for librarians throughout the country interested in serving incarcerated populations.[23] The listserv included 565 members as of April 2024, an average of 11 members per state, including Puerto Rico.[24] The LSJI site *prison-l@cvl-lists.org* is described as a resource for

> library professionals, students, correctional staff, volunteers, or anyone who serves the underserved in correctional settings (prison, jail, detention centers, state mental health institutes, juvenile facilities) or justice-involved individuals (those in halfway houses, community corrections, sober living, transitional housing, on parole, or the formerly incarcerated).

Listserv owners may be contacted by email: *prison-l-owner@cvl-lists.org*. A directory of state prison libraries, as well as other library resources, is maintained by the Washington State Library Institutional Library Services Staff.[25]

The International Federation of Library Associations and Institutions (IFLA) is a "global voice of the library and information profession" (Krolak, 2019, p. 20). Its Working Group on Prison Libraries, established in 2019, serves to maintain the IFLA Guidelines for Library Services to Prisoners,[26] an Action Plan for the Working Group,[27] a Bibliography,[28] research documents and tools,[29] and an email listserv.[30] The site *prison-l@iflalists.org* is described as a Prison Libraries Working Group Discussion List, public, but restricted to subscribers. The list, moderated by the Chair of the IFLA Working Group on Prison Libraries within the framework of the IFLA Library Services to People with Special Needs Section (LSN), supports those offering services to prisoners. The site is open to all individuals, institutions, and organizations. More information can be found at: www.ifla.org/node/92564.

Lisa Krolak has been a leader in IFLA as chair of the global working group on prison libraries, within the IFLA Section for Library Services to People with Special Needs. In that capacity, she was instrumental in updating IFLA Guidelines on Prison Libraries. Since 2001, she has been the chief librarian at the UNESCO Institute for Lifelong Learning in Hamburg, Germany.[31] She has a diploma in librarianship from Germany and an M.Sc. in information and library studies from the United Kingdom.

Functional category: Library

Mellon Foundation

The multi-billion dollar Andrew W. Mellon Foundation, or the Mellon Foundation, was founded in 1969 and is, according to its website, the largest funder of arts and humanities in the nation.[32] With over $8 billion in assets in 2022, the foundation expended over $500 million in contributions, gifts, and grants.

In February 2024, the Mellon Foundation and Haymarket Books[33] announced the first annual Writing Freedom Fellows, 20 writers affected by the carceral system who will receive support for authoring works of poetry, fiction, and creative nonfiction. The Writing Freedom Fellowship was established by Haymarket, a nonprofit publisher, with support from Mellon and the now-closed Art for Justice project. The Fellows may write on any topic, not necessarily related to the carceral system, and receive mentorship and professional development as well as a monetary award.[34]

The President of the Mellon Foundation, Dr. Elizabeth Alexander, is an expert on race, justice, the arts, and society in the United States and has been a leader in providing support to many of the organizations described here. Alexander previously served at the Ford Foundation, where she codesigned their Art for Justice Fund, combining advocacy with art to address mass incarceration.

Functional category: Logistics

The MIT Educational Justice Institute

With respect to promoting education in prison, The Educational Justice Institute, MIT (TEJI), established in 2018 is a leader in raising the quality of life in prison through education, particularly through the use of technology to impart digital literacy skills in preparation for eventual re-entry to the community.[35] TEJI also engages students at MIT in programs that raise their awareness of issues of mass incarceration. Dr. Lee Perlman and Carole Cafferty joined forces to create TEJI and also founded and manage the Massachusetts Prison Education Consortium (MPEC) to support post-secondary education for residents in prison and formerly incarcerated people with funding from the Mellon Foundation administered by The Vera Institute of Justice.

Dr. Lee Perlman earned his doctorate from MIT in political philosophy. His teaching experience in prisons dates to 2012, when he taught through Boston University's Prison Education Program, and continued to teach through the MIT Prison Initiative, which he founded in 2016. Carole Cafferty brings invaluable experience from over 30 years of correctional service, including her last position before retirement as Superintendent of a corrections facility in Massachusetts. She earned a master's degree in Correctional Administration from the University of Massachusetts in Lowell, where she teaches in the School of Criminology and Justice Studies.

See "We, The Unbound," an augmented reality mural created as a collaboration between artists at MIT and The Suffolk County House of Correction here: www.teji.mit.edu/projects.

Functional category: Logistics

Museum for Black Innovation and Entrepreneurship

Founded in 2011 in Washington, DC, the Museum for Black Innovation and Entrepreneurship (MBIE) aims to be a catalyst for inspiring Black and other underserved residents in Wards 7 and 8 sections of the nation's capital by showcasing exemplars of Black creativity.[36] I co-founded MBIE with the Reverend Dr. Kendrick Curry, senior pastor at the Pennsylvania Baptist Church, who serves as board chair with members Dr. Patricia Sluby, a prolific researcher and author on Black innovation and entrepreneurship (Sluby, 2004, 2011), and psychiatrist Kevin Williams, M.D., who is also an inventor with an MBA degree.

MBIE-related efforts have resulted in hosting a community exhibit in Washington, DC, the creation of short videos on community perceptions of intellectual property available online,[37] preparation of handbooks for educators and librarians around the country to promote understanding of Black innovation and entrepreneurship (Whitman, 2017/2020, 2019), and various publications on the topic of IP and social justice, including addressing people in prison (Mtima & Whitman, 2022; Whitman, 2015, 2024b).

Functional category: Logistics

PEN America's Prison and Justice Writing Program

The leading champion for promoting literary works by writers in detention is PEN America's Prison and Justice Writing Program, which began in 1960 as the Writers in Prison program.[38] Resources and programs include handbooks for incarcerated writers (Aiello & Taylor, 2005; Meissner, 2022), distributed at no cost to prisons throughout the country, a prison writing contest resulting in a published anthology, a mentorship program pairing professional authors with writers in prison, a Writing for Justice fellowship, and an online literary series and podcast. Under the leadership of Dr. Moira Marquis, the Prison and Justice Writing Program's Freewrite Project at PEN America produced *A Writer's Workshop Curriculum Guide* and a facilitator's companion guide (PEN America, 2024a, 2024b).

Lateef Mtima and I contributed a chapter on protecting intellectual property to the PEN prison writing handbook, *The Sentences That Create Us* (Meissner, 2022; Mtima & Whitman, 2022), and I was engaged to help match the work of artists in prison with writers in prison for a special anthology compiled with Wendy Jason of JAC, *Breathe Into the Ground* (Meissner, 2021).

Functional category: Production (literature) and Intermediation

The Pollen Initiative

The Pollen Initiative was organized after founder Jesse Vasquez's incarceration in 2017 to develop media centers inside prisons and jails in America.[39] Residents participating in the program engage in journalism and audiovisual training in order to tell stories that provide readers with an understanding of the carceral system based on authentic sources. The Pollen Initiative reports zero recidivism to date among its participants.

Vasquez was editor-in-chief of the *San Quentin News* from 2017 to 2019, when he was paroled. Kate McQueen, formerly managing editor of the PJP's instructional newspaper and PJP's Prison Newspaper Project, is the editorial director of the Initiative. She has a Ph.D. in literature from Stanford University and a master's degree in journalism from the University of Illinois Urbana-Champaign. She is on the faculty at the University of California Santa Cruz. Her website provides links to her media appearances.[40]

Functional category: Production (literature) and Intermediation

Prison Journalism Project

The PJP aims to equip writers in prison with the means to become journalists who can contribute to shaping the carceral system.[41] Founded and led by Yukari Iwatani Kane, with boards of esteemed directors and advisors, PJP is in the process of building a national network of prison correspondents. PJP provides interested residents with writing guides, including a guide to starting a prison publication,[42] a newsletter, a newspaper, and training tips. Writers who have demonstrated strengths are invited to become contributors and are eligible for mentorship through a journalism correspondence program. PJP is also working with the Society of Professional Journalists to create a national chapter of incarcerated journalists. As of April 2024, PJP had engaged 735 writers in 239 prisons in 41 states and three countries, posting some 2,280 stories.

Founder Yukari Kane has worked as a journalist for over two decades and served as a staff writer for *The Wall Street Journal* and Reuters. While teaching at San Quentin State Prison, she created a prison journalism curriculum. She engaged as a fellow in the 2024 CUNY Executive Program in News Innovation and Leadership, is an advisory council member of the News Literacy Project, an advisor for the San Quentin News, and an advisor to a prison newspaper at Everglades Correctional Institution in Florida.

Functional category: Production (literature) and Intermediation

Prison Studies Project

The mission of the Prison Studies Project (PSP) at Harvard University is "to awaken the broadest possible public to the ways we punish, and to reimagine justice in the United States."[43] Founded in 2008 by Kaia Stern and Bruce Western, PSP focuses on research, education, and policy change by raising public awareness and teaching college courses. PSP has compiled a directory of programs of higher education in prison, the *National Directory of Higher Education Programs in Prison*, in partnership with the Alliance for Higher Education in Prison.[44]

PSP has also partnered with Harvard Law School and the Harvard Graduate School of Education in the Transforming Justice Initiative to conduct community conversations, including through public forums, some held in jails and prisons, films, and lunch sessions with students. In 2022, PSP, the Harvard Radcliffe Institute for Advanced Study,[45] and the Center for Cartoon Studies[46] convened a two-year public education campaign called Why We Punish to generate discussions about punishment in the United States, beginning with a 32-page comic book on mass incarceration serving as the first of several materials designed for civic learning.

Dr. Kaia Stern has worked with numerous organizations over a 25-year period, including the Greenhaven Prison Program at Vassar College, neighborhood Defender Service of Harlem, Vera Institute of Justice, and the Open Society Institute, and is the author of *Voices from American Prisons: Faith, Education and Healing* (Stern, 2014). Stern, ordained as an interfaith minister, received her doctorate in religion from Emory University and M.A. in theological studies from the Harvard Divinity School.

Dr. Bruce Western is Bryce professor of sociology and social justice and co-director of the Justice Lab at Columbia University. He is the author of *Homeward: Life in the Year After Prison* (Russell Sage Foundation, 2018) and *Punishment and Inequality in America* (Russell Sage Foundation, 2006).

Western, born in Australia, received his Ph.D. in sociology from the University of California, Los Angeles.

Functional category: Logistics

Rehabilitation Through the Arts

RTA has been reducing recidivism in the New York prison population since 1996, achieving a rate that is now reportedly less than 3%, compared to a national rate of over 60% within three years.[47] RTA operates in eight medium to maximum security facilities for men and women. The program's success is featured in the film, "Sing Sing."[48] RTA's mission, posted on its website, is to help "people in prison develop critical life skills through the arts, modeling an approach to the justice system based on human dignity rather than punishment," and its values include "dignity, creativity, commitment, and collaboration."

Following a visit to Sing Sing with her husband, Hans Hallundbaek, Katherine Vockins founded RTA with resident Talib Amir Muhammad to engage professional teaching artists to conduct year-round workshops in theater, dance, music, creative writing, and visual arts. Each program engages residents in a non-judgmental community of peers, all of whom discover new possibilities for themselves by learning critical life skills through the arts.

Functional category: Production

San Francisco Public Library (SFPL)

According to its website, librarians at the San Francisco Public Library (SFPL) have provided services to juvenile detention centers and jails and conducted research on library services in carceral facilities since about 2010. In 2018, the Jail and Re-entry Services (JARS) program began providing services to adults in detention. The SFPL also produces white papers on extending information access to incarcerated people (Austin et al., 2023).

Dr. Jeanie Austin is a leader in the movement to provide library services to the incarcerated based at the SFPL JARS program.[49] They earned their Ph.D. in library and information science at the University of Illinois at Urbana-Champaign. They are a jail and re-entry services librarian at the SFPL and co-principal investigator on the Mellon Foundation-funded Expanding Information Access for Incarcerated People grant. In addition to authoring numerous journal articles, their book *Library Services and Incarceration: Recognizing Barriers, Strengthening Access* was published by the ALA (Austin, 2022).

Functional category: Library

Shakespeare Behind Bars

Shakespeare Behind Bars (SBB), according to its website, was founded by Curt L. Tofteland in 1995 and is now the "oldest, continuously operating program of its kind in North America."[50] Its mission, stated on its website, is "to offer theatrical encounters with personal and social issues to incarcerated, post-incarcerated, marginalized, and at-risk communities, allowing them to develop and expand life skills that will support their reintegration into society."

SBB's philosophy according to its website

> is that all citizens, incarcerated or not, have an authentic voice that is their strength. This voice can find renewed relationships to self and society through art, theatre (specifically . . . the collected works of William Shakespeare), and original writing,

a statement that also serves as a subtext to this book. SBB's website reports that its recidivism rate of 6% is far lower than the national average of 68%. Shakespeare Beyond Bars is an online discussion venue for returning citizens who took part in SBB during their incarcerated years. Larry Brewster, cited several times in this book, participates in this program.

Curt L. Tofteland is a prison arts practitioner with over 40 years of theater experience as a professional. He began SBB in Kentucky and later launched a program in Michigan. He has given talks throughout the country and internationally. He is also a poet and essayist, with a number of published works, a four-time speaker on TEDx Talks, and has received numerous awards for his pioneering work.

Functional category: Production (literature)

William James Association

WJA, founded by Page Smith and Paul Lee in 1973, is named after the American philosopher who espoused service work in place of military service.[51] In 1973, WJA launched the Prison Arts Project to provide arts experience to thousands of men, women, and youth in detention, and in 2009 adopted the Poetic Justice Project, which promotes theater as a means to examine crime, punishment, and redemption. According to its website, WJA espouses a commitment to humanizing language, repudiating dehumanizing terms such as "inmates, criminals, prisoners, convicts, delinquents, felons, and offenders," and instead advises using words to reference people that "reflect their full identities, and acknowledge their capacity to change and grow."[52]

Laurie Brooks, a ceramics artist, has led WJA since 2001. According to her LinkedIn page, she has facilitated arts-in-corrections efforts since 1989, collaborated with the California Arts Council and other groups in the 1990s, helped develop programs for the California Youth Authority and Arts in Mental Health, and has spent 15 years working with the National Endowment for the Arts Office of Accessibility to base arts-in-residence programs in Federal Bureau of Prisons facilities. Laurie has a degree in Economics and Community Studies from the University of California, Santa Cruz, and is on the Board of Directors of the Cultural Council of Santa Cruz County.

Functional category: Production and Logistics

▪ ▪ ▪

These organizations and their leaders are among the brightest lights facilitating creativity in detention and serving as intermediaries for the national dissemination of creative works. While some collaborate, many operate independently and prefer to do so.

How might we imagine a more strategic, national framework in which such groups, these or others not included here, continue to not only operate with sovereignty but also benefit from being a part of a larger confederation, leveraging their respective assets to achieve a common goal? Is there an opportunity to scale the benefits of a carceral creativity policy by integrating and building on such existing programs?

Notes

1 See: https://ww2.americansforthearts.org/publications, cited 12 February 2024.
2 See: https://artforjusticefund.org/, cited 13 July 2024.
3 See: https://thejusticeartscoalition.org/programs/, cited 12 February 2024.
4 See: https://apaep.auburn.edu/, cited 13 March 2024.
5 See: www.prisonpolicy.org/profiles/AL.html, cited 13 March 2024.
6 See: https://prisonwitness.org/, cited 15 February 2024.
7 See: https://artforjusticefund.org/, cited 15 February 2024.
8 See: https://artforjusticefund.org/resources/, cited 5 May 2024.
9 See: www.calawyersforthearts.org/about.html, cited 15 February 2024.
10 See: www.americansforthearts.org/by-program/promotion-and-recognition/awards-for-arts-achievement/annual-awards/michael-newton-award/alma-robinson, cited 15 February 2024.
11 See: https://copyrightalliance.org/, cited 26 April 2024.
12 I have been a member since September 2020.
13 See: www.earhustlesq.com/, cited 15 May 2024.
14 See: www.firststepalliance.org/, cited 23 April 2024.
15 See: www.freerrecords.com/, cited 15 February 2024.
16 See: https://vimeo.com/10140709, cited 15 February 2024.
17 See: https://iipsj.org/, cited 15 February 2024.
18 See: https://youtu.be/Um3q3mHAEIs?feature=shared, cited 4 April 2024.
19 See: www.jailguitardoors.org.uk/, cited 19 February 2024.
20 See: https://jail-guitar-doors.myshopify.com/, cited 19 February 2024.

21 See: https://thejusticeartscoalition.org/, cited 15 February 2024.
22 See: https://libguides.ala.org/PrisonLibraries, cited 15 February 2024.
23 See: www.cvl-lists.org/mailman3/postorius/lists/ @cvl-lists.org/, cited 15 February 2024.
24 Personal correspondence, Chelsea Jordan-Makely, 8 April 2024.
25 See: https://washstatelib.libguides.com/directoryofstateprisonlibraries/home, cited 8 April 2024.
26 See: https://repository.ifla.org/handle/123456789/2538, cited 8 April 2024.
27 See: www.ifla.org/wp-content/uploads/ActionPlan_PrisonLibraries_March 2022.pdf, cited 8 April 2024.
28 See: www.ifla.org/wp-content/uploads/Bibliography_PrisonLibraries_March 2023.pdf, cited 8 April 2024.
29 See: www.ifla.org/files/assets/lsn/publications/workingtools_prisonlibraries.pdf, cited 8 April 2024.
30 See: https://mail.iflalists.org/wws/info/prison-l, cited 8 March 2024.
31 See: www.uil.unesco.org/en, cited 19 July 2024.
32 See: www.mellon.org/, cited 13 July 2024.
33 See: www.haymarketbooks.org/, cited 13 March 2024. Haymarket Books takes its name from the Chicago bombing event on 4 May 1886 in Haymarket Square, for which eight men, the "Haymarket Martyrs," were imprisoned for expressing their views (Neier, 1995/1998, p. 355), www.haymarketbooks.org/pg/about, cited 15 March 2024.
34 See: www.mellon.org/news/haymarket-books-mellon-foundation-writing-freedom-fellowship, cited 13 March 2024.
35 See: www.teji.mit.edu/, cited 8 March 2024.
36 See: https://mbiedc.org/, cited 5 May 2024.
37 See: https://mbiedc.org/styled-7-videos/videos.html, cited 5 May 2024.
38 See: https://pen.org/prison-writing/, cited 15 February 2024.
39 See: https://polleninitiative.org/, cited 26 June 2024.
40 See: https://katejoymcqueen.com/, cited 26 June 2024.
41 See: https://prisonjournalismproject.org/ and https://prisonjournalismproject.org/prison-newspaper-project/, cited 26 June 2024.
42 https://drive.google.com/file/d/1OjlCq_Jnon4vEcGNHugcJFxb_40gEMeX/view, cited 26 June 2024.
43 See: https://prisonstudiesproject.org/, cited 28 April 2024.
44 See: www.higheredinprison.org/, cited 28 April 2024.
45 See: www.radcliffe.harvard.edu/, cited 28 April 2024.
46 See: www.cartoonstudies.org/, cited 28 April 2024.
47 See: https://rta-arts.org/, cited 8 July 2024.
48 See: https://en.wikipedia.org/wiki/Sing_Sing_(2023_film), cited 19 July 2024.
49 See: https://sfpl.org/services/jail-and-reentry-services, cited 15 February 2024.
50 See: https://shakespearebehindbars.org/, cited 20 March 2024.
51 See: https://williamjamesassociation.org/, cited 19 February 2024.
52 See: https://williamjamesassociation.org/our-mission-vision-values/#, cited 19 February 2024.

References

Aiello, A., & Taylor, J. (2005). *Handbook for writers in prison*. PEN America Center.

Alexander, M. (2010/2012). *The new Jim Crow: Mass incarceration in the age of colorblindness*. The New Press.

Austin, J. (2022). *Library services and incarceration: Recognizing barriers, strengthening access*. ALA and Neal Schuman.

Austin, J., Kinnon, R., Ness, N., & Okelo, B. (2023). *Technology in carceral facilities: Trends, limitations, and opportunities for libraries*. San Francisco Public Library Jail and Reentry Services program.

Brewster, L., & Merts, P. (2015). *Paths of discovery: Art practice and its impact in California prisons* (2nd ed.). Self Published.

Bulgren, C. W. (2020). Jail Guitar Doors: A case study of guitar and songwriting instruction in Cook County Jail. *International Journal of Community Music*, *13*(3), 299–318. https://doi.org/10.1386/ijcm_00026_1

Du Vernay, A. (2016). 13th. *Netflix Studios*. www.youtube.com/watch?v=krfcq5pF8u8 cited 18 January 2024.

Gardner, A., Hager, L. L., & Hillman, G. (2014). *Prison arts resource project: An annotated bibliography*. National Endowment for the Arts. www.americansforthearts.org/node/100823 cited 23 January 2024.

Grunenwald, J. (2019). *Reading behind bars: A true story of literature, law, and life as a prison librarian*. Skyhorse Publishing.

Hillman, G. (2023). *Arts in corrections: Thirty years of annotated publications*. Routledge.

Jamar, S. D., & Mtima, L. (Eds.). (2024). *The Cambridge handbook of intellectual property and social justice*. Cambridge University Press.

Kaushal, A., Ladha, T., & Silberman, D. (2021). *Financial health and criminal justice: The impacts of involvement*. Financial Health Network.

Keller, B. (2022). *What's prison for? Punishment and rehabilitation in the age of mass incarceration*. Columbia Global Reports.

Krolak, L. (2019). *Books beyond bars: The transformative potential of prison libraries*. UNESCO Institute for Lifelong Learning. http://uil.unesco.org/adult-education/books-beyond-bars-transformative-potential-prison-libraries cited 10 February 2020.

Larson, D. (Ed.). (2013). *Fourth city: Essays from the prison in America*. Michigan State University Press.

Larson, D. (2024). *Inside knowledge: Incarcerated people on the failures of the American prison*. New York University Press.

Meissner, C. (Ed.). (2021). *Breathe into the ground: PEN America prison writing anthology*. PEN America.

Meissner, C. (Ed.). (2022). *The sentences that create us: Crafting a writer's life in prison*. Haymarket Books.

Moffat, V. R. (2023). The free exercise of copyright behind bars. *Washington and Lee Law Review*, *80*(2), 741–802.

Mtima, L., & Whitman, J. R. (2022). Copyright protection in brief. In C. Meissner (Ed.), *The sentences that create us: Crafting a writer's life in prison*. Haymarket Books.

Neier, A. (1995/1998). Confining dissent: The political prison. In N. Morris & D. J. Rothman (Eds.), *The Oxford history of prison: The practice of punishment in western society* (pp. 350–380). Oxford University Press.

PEN America. (2024a). *The Freewrite Project: A writer's workshop curriculum guide*. Prison and Justice Writing, PEN America.

PEN America. (2024b). *The Freewrite Project: A writer's workshop curriculum guide, facilitator's guide*. Prison and Justice Writing, PEN America.

Sluby, P. C. (2004). *The inventive spirit of African Americans: Patented ingenuity*. Praeger Publishers.

Sluby, P. C. (2011). *The entrepreneurial spirit of African American inventors*. Praeger.

Stern, K. (2014). *Voices from American prisons: Faith, education, and healing*. Routledge.

Stevenson, B. (2014). *Just mercy*. Spiegel & Grau.

Watson, S. (2019). *Economic wellbeing of U.S. adults with experiences with incarceration and unpaid legal costs*. First Step Alliance.

Whitman, J. R. (2015). An entrepreneurship approach to achieving IP social justice. In L. Mtima (Ed.), *Intellectual property, entrepreneurship and social justice: From swords to ploughshares* (pp. 33–63). Edward Elgar Publishing, Inc. https://doi.org/10.4337/9781783470259.00009

Whitman, J. R. (2017/2020). *IPFI handbook for librarians and educators: Assisting creators to protect and share their intellectual property* (3rd ed.). Museum for Black Innovation and Entrepreneurship.

Whitman, J. R. (2019). *MBIE for librarians: A handbook assisting librarians to highlight Black innovation and entrepreneurship*. Museum for Black Innovation and Entrepreneurship.

Whitman, J. R. (2024a). Inside knowledge [book review]. *Howard Journal of Crime and Justice*. https://doi.org/10.1111/hojo.12553

Whitman, J. R. (2024b). Intellectual property empowerment and protection for prisoners. In S. Jamar & L. Mtima (Eds.), *Handbook of intellectual property and social justice* (pp. 245–264). Cambridge University Press. https://doi.org/10.1017/9781108697613

Williams, R. L. (2023). Good writing in a bad place: How one incarcerated writer feeds his craft. *Literary Hub*. https://lithub.com/good-writing-in-a-bad-place-how-one-incarcerated-writer-feeds-his-craft/ cited 28 August 2023.

7 A Nationwide Carceral Creativity Framework

Creators in prison represent the supply side of a prison creativity enterprise. Considering the *demand side*, if you were an art collector in search of works created by people in prison, where would you turn? You might search the internet. Which sources are reputable? Checking with the Better Business Bureau is always a good idea. To date, the market consists of a somewhat motley distribution of for-profit and nonprofit players largely specializing in a single modality, such as visual art, writing, or music, and there is no trustworthy, quality-controlled, integrated marketplace organized for buying or selling works in any artistic mode created by people in prisons.

But, applying an entrepreneurial approach to achieving social justice (Whitman, 2015), there could be. And I think an integrated framework of reputable arts intermediaries would offer several benefits. First, it is difficult for one residing in prison to be able to search for a reliable outlet for one's creative work. Through the admirable leadership of Wendy Jason, the JAC built relationships with a number of visual artists who express deep gratitude for how Wendy represented their work. Jason set an example of how a larger, more integrated, multi-modal framework might work. The APWA and FREER Records have also established strong reputations in writing and music recording, respectively.

Second, if residents in detention knew there was a marketplace for their creative works, and that access to the market was feasible, they might be more motivated to produce such works for public benefit, in effect, moving what I call "dark IP" into the light. Third, if the public were aware of a trustworthy source of creative works emanating from prisons, potential buyers might take a greater interest in viewing such works for possible purchase. Additionally, an established nonprofit organization serving as the "backbone" for such intermediaries could be a reliable partner for working with correctional facilities to identify quality arts-in-corrections teachers and educational programs.

DOI: 10.4324/9781003566021-8

But to date, the various players are not yet integrated into a collaborative framework that could be positioned and branded to deliver these benefits. The following notes outline the elements of a proposed Nationwide Carceral Creativity Framework to encourage further exploration and discussion of the concept among all interested players.

Teachers

Qualified teachers are essential to promoting wide-scale engagement in creative work on the inside. Individual residents in prisons are self-taught or may have arrived with prior training in artistic skills, and they may be independently engaged in creating works. This is the norm for many artists, writers, and musicians working in detention. Their work should be encouraged and supported. However, a creative carceral policy would promote the initiation of a far more inclusive effort to engage many more residents in creative work. This would typically involve contracting with individual teachers or arts-in-corrections programs prepared to help residents learn and develop creative and life skills.

The importance of educators in arts-in-corrections and the role they play in helping residents learn the disciplines of writing, creating visual arts, composing music, and other skills cannot be overstated. The commitment to student success on the inside and preparation for the unique needs of incarcerated studies is crucial. I quote here from one educator with over two decades of teaching on the inside, who chooses to remain anonymous (personal communication, May 14, 2024):

> My own take on prison education is that it develops my students' capacities in many ways. Their self-esteem is positively affected when they experience success in class. Everything that they take away from class – the learning itself and all of the by-products – helps them when they are released, because the experience of being in a trusted community of fellow learners gives them exposure and confidence . . .. I have seen that programs like culinary and cosmetology in combination with what I teach (fiction, college writing, poetry, and the like) give them a sense of well-being, rounded and marketable. They see what education can do for them.

But, this educator argues, proper preparation for teaching in a prison context is essential for success (personal communication, May 14, 2024):

> I maintain that someone who works with incarcerated folks needs to know something about trauma and also about how to reach folks who may initially be reticent to trust . . .. Students have more success with professors

who know how to invite them into the work in a way that is welcoming.... I've also found that teaching writing is a process. It's important to help students find their niche and help them to grow, beginning by establishing trust. I work in another job that I have with a man who is an excellent spoken word poet and he's also an actor. However, I would NEVER bring him to meet my female students because he is not well enough equipped to know how to work with incarcerated women. He thinks he knows a lot about trauma but I think he'd cause harm rather than good.

Concerns such as those indicated earlier underscore the importance of setting high teaching standards and ensuring that educational participants are suitably prepared for offering instruction in a carceral facility. The role of arts-in-corrections is central to the proposed national framework, for through such programs more people in prison will be able to develop and exercise their creative skills on the supply side of carceral creativity. To facilitate the demand side for creative works, we turn to the framework. I have not yet discussed the framework with the organizations listed, and some would likely not be interested in joining. But I take the liberty of citing these organizations purely as placeholders for the types of capabilities that could contribute to a Carceral Creativity Framework.

The Framework

The following figure illustrates a propositional nationwide framework for protecting and disseminating works created in prisons in a more rationalized and quality-controlled way to protect and benefit people in prison. The framework connects supply and demand. The framework, in effect, identifies and links together relevant elements, in this case related to prison, in the larger, national creativity ecosystem, in which creative works have a life cycle that can be traced from gestation to fabrication, to distribution, and to consumption.

Its proposed mission is: *To motivate the creation of expressive works by people in prison, to protect ownership of their works, and to disseminate these works to the public.*

Organizations such as those described in the previous chapter would be invited to pursue this mission through the framework on a voluntary, collaborative basis. The following table shows how the programs in the previous chapter, included here for illustrative purposes only, might be arranged in a framework according to their capability.

Framework-related functions provided by participating organizations would be coordinated by a backbone organization. A "backbone" nonprofit organization is an independent entity capable of raising funds for an interdisciplinary program that engages multiple organizations with diverse capabilities to achieve a common goal, thus achieving a "collective impact"

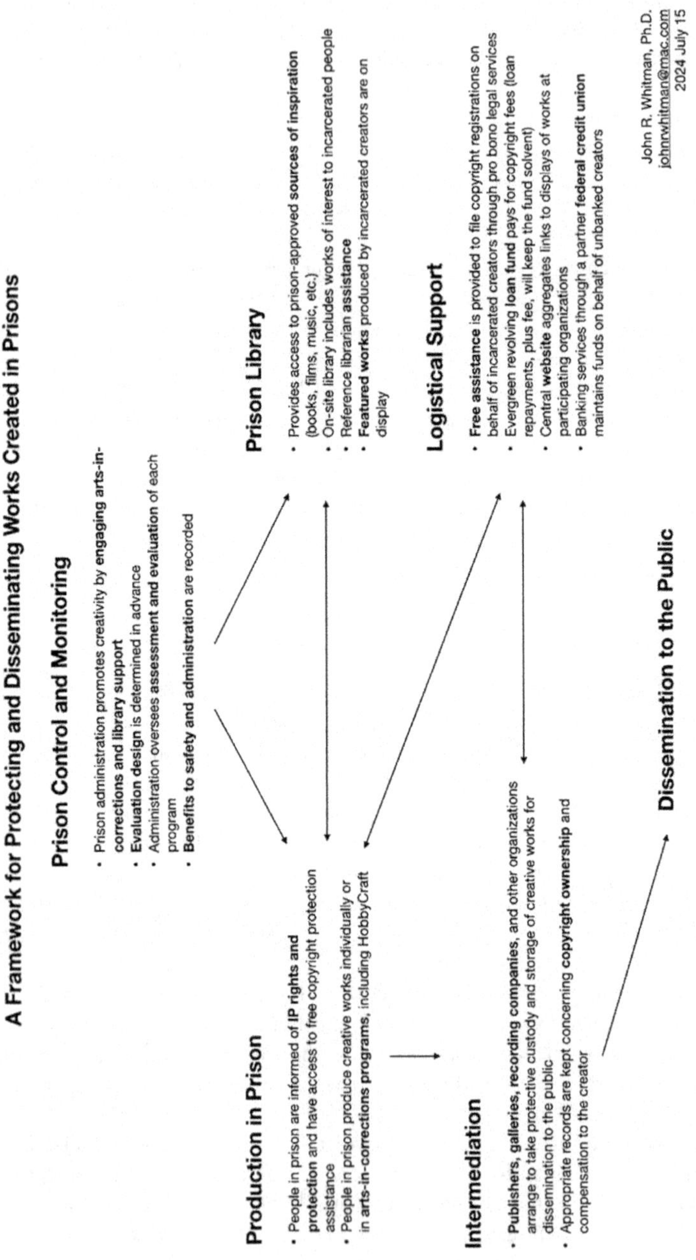

A Framework for Protecting and Disseminating Works Created in Prisons

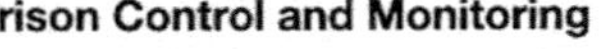

Prison Control and Monitoring

- Prison administration promotes creativity by **engaging arts-in-corrections and library support**
- **Evaluation design** is determined in advance
- Administration oversees **assessment and evaluation** of each program
- **Benefits to safety and administration** are recorded

Production in Prison

- People in prison are informed of **IP rights and protection** and have access to free copyright protection assistance
- People in prison produce creative works individually or in **arts-in-corrections programs**, including HobbyCraft

Prison Library

- Provides access to prison-approved **sources of inspiration** (books, films, music, etc.)
- On-site library includes works of interest to incarcerated people
- Reference librarian **assistance**
- **Featured works** produced by incarcerated creators are on display

Intermediation

- **Publishers, galleries, recording companies**, and other organizations arrange to take protective custody and storage of creative works for dissemination to the public
- Appropriate records are kept concerning **copyright ownership** and compensation to the creator

Logistical Support

- **Free assistance** is provided to file copyright registrations on behalf of incarcerated creators through pro bono legal services
- Evergreen revolving **loan fund** pays for copyright fees (loan repayments, plus fee, will keep the fund solvent)
- Central **website** aggregates links to displays of works at participating organizations
- Banking services through a partner **federal credit union** maintains funds on behalf of unbanked creators

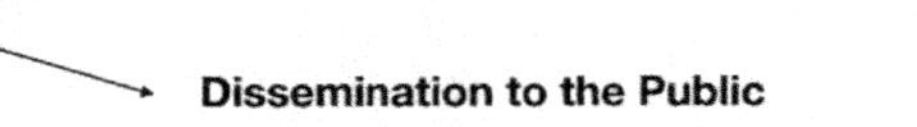

Dissemination to the Public

John R. Whitman, Ph.D.
johnrwhitman@mac.com
2024 July 15

Figure 7.1 A national framework for dissemination.

Table 7.1 Framework Capabilities Matrix

Program	*Production*				*Library*	*Inter-mediation*	*Logistics*
	Writing	*Visual Art*	*Music*	*Other*			
Alabama Prison Arts and Education Project	1					1	
American Prison Writing Archive	1					1	
Art for Justice Fund							1
California Lawyers for the Arts							1
Copyright Alliance							1
Ear Hustle						1	
First Step Alliance							1
FREER Records			1			1	
Institute for Intellectual Property and Social Justice							
Jail Guitar Doors			1				
Justice Arts Coalition	1	1				1	
American Library Association/IFLA					1		1
Mellon Foundation							1
MIT Educational Justice Initiative							1
Museum for Black Innovation and Entrepreneurship							1
PEN America	1					1	
Pollen Initiative	1					1	
Prison Journalism Project	1					1	
Prison Studies Project							1
Rehabilitation Through the Arts	1	1	1	1			
San Francisco Public Library					1		
Shakespeare Behind Bars				1			
William James Association		1					1
TOTALS	7	3	3	3	2	8	11

(Hanleybrown et al., 2012; Kania & Kramer, 2011). Such an independent non-profit backbone organization, once formed and funded and advised by a board including corrections professionals and formerly incarcerated creators, would build and maintain the proposed nationwide framework. Organizations would be invited to join the program and benefit from it, at no cost to them. Indeed, the backbone organization could facilitate raising funds to build capacity in such organizations to better serve the collective mission. Levels and sources of funding are being explored.

Production in Prison

These organizations would ensure the protection of resident IP rights and engage them in learning skills for creative endeavors. Arts-in-corrections programs would engage residents in learning the skills of creativity. Such educational programs may be seen as vocational training in that they impart and build skills that would be highly useful following re-entry to the community, even among residents who go on to other types of employment. Learning artistic skills also imparts values and life skills of concentration and hard work, constructive engagement with others and reduced tension, and self-reflection and discovery (Brewster, 1983, 2014). Arts-in-corrections programs are exemplified by the Alabama Prison Arts and Education Project, Jail Guitar Doors, Shakespeare Behind Bars, as well as many other projects long supported by organizations such as Art for Justice Fund, California Lawyers for the Arts, Mellon Foundation, MIT Educational Justice Institute, and William James Association.

Arts-in-corrections programs help participants to cope with trauma, strengthen relationships with their families, and build connections to the community (Eason et al., 2021). As prison observers Larry Brewster and Peter Merts have noted, successful community reintegration is the ultimate goal of corrections (Brewster & Merts, 2015, p. 165). A RAND meta-analysis of prison educational programs indicates they cost-effectively reduce recidivism (Davis et al., 2013).

Prison Library

Related to life-long learning would be the role of libraries, preferably located within prisons, for libraries can provide materials that inspire creativity in ways not otherwise accessible to residents living in Spartan conditions. Prison librarianship, according to librarian and author Jeanie Austin, has been somewhat overlooked as a niche service deserving greater attention (Austin, 2022, p. xiii). The role of prison libraries to provide transformative benefits to residents is described in *Books Beyond Bars*, by Lisa Krolak of the UNESCO Institute for Lifelong Learning (Krolak, 2019). Libraries could also feature works done by people in prison.

Libraries such as the SFPL and associations like the American Library Association may provide invaluable guidance on creating a library capacity to meet creative needs beyond the requisite materials for a law library.

Intermediation

Other organizations would include intermediary marketers and distributors of creative works by people in prison, including publishing agents, publishers, art galleries, music recording studios, and other nonprofit organizations engaged in promoting creativity in prisons. An intermediary group that accepts visual art from residents for display and possible sale, may require funding for a larger space for storing such works and a computer-based system for tracking them.

The feasibility of such a framework would depend on individual prison residents and especially prison superintendents interested in participating in such a program. For they would provide the supply of creative works for dissemination to the public. Residents and/or each facility would select among participating intermediary organizations depending on need. Participating programs would be screened by the backbone organization for quality control as part of eligibility to take part in the program. Without screening, we cannot be sure that organizations and their leadership are credible or well-organized. In an interview with Alex Greenberger, editor of ARTnews, Nicole R. Fleetwood, author of *Marking Time: Art in the Age of Mass Incarceration*, recounted stories of art confiscation, loss, and the risk of working with unaccountable individuals or groups (Greenberger, 2020, July 8).

Incarcerated people have no bargaining power when faced with the prospect of distributing their creations through commercial, or even nonprofit distribution networks. Publishers, art galleries, or record labels are typically controlled by cultural "gatekeepers" who make selections based on their own cultural tastes and possible racial, ethnic, and social class biases. Creators in prison are highly vulnerable to exploitation, just as Blacks and other marginalized creators in the general population have experienced (Mtima, 2024, p. 117). I cannot stress enough the need for trust and accountability in such a framework for creating and disseminating carceral creations.

Logistical Support

Pro bono assistance should be available for copyright registration and payment of copyright registration fees. New capabilities would also be required. Specifically, the backbone organization would open a new website with links to the participating publishers, galleries, and recording studios featuring works from prison. This would provide a one-stop online source to find vetted and protected works from prison creators. The backbone organization would not directly engage in buying and selling; such transactions would continue directly between the creators, participating organizations, and their customers.

The backbone organization would also establish, possibly in collaboration with an organization like the Copyright Alliance, an "evergreen revolving fund" to advance copyright registration fees that creators are unable to pay at the time of registration. To be clear, creators own the copyright to their work once it is affixed to some medium (such as paper, canvas, clay, a recording medium, etc.), and while I would encourage the creator to put his or her name and the word "copyright" or the symbol © on each work, registration is voluntary (Mtima & Whitman, 2022). But to be able to enforce ownership by bringing an infringement lawsuit, the work requires registration with the U.S. Copyright Office, and it is best to do so if the work might have financial value in the market. Lacking the financial resources to register a copyright should never be a barrier to exercising the right to apply for registration. Successful creators could then repay such fees to the evergreen fund, keeping it solvent for ongoing needs.

Additionally, the backbone organization would seek to partner with a federal credit union, such as that being established by First Step Alliance,[1] to maintain accounts for unbanked people while in prison and following community re-entry. Credit unions are member-owned, nonprofit organizations. Their bylaws indicate the common attributes that define membership, whether by community, association, or occupation. Justice-impacted individuals would be eligible to join a credit union by virtue of their free membership in a common association such as FSA. Each creator, as an account holder, would instruct a gallery or publisher to deposit proceeds from sales to the creator's credit union account and the creator or his or her designated representative, such as a family member, would control the distribution of any funds from the account. The advantage of a federal credit union is that membership could be nationwide.

Dissemination

Dissemination of works to the public can take a variety of forms. Literary works may be acquired, printed, and distributed by magazine or book publishers, or by more scholarly projects such as the APWA or advocacy organizations like PEN America. Visual arts may be displayed by galleries and sold to customers. Musical compositions may be recorded and published by an organization like FREER Records.

Evaluation

Of course, any such framework program should be subject to evaluation. A plan for program evaluation should advisedly be prepared well in advance of launching the program and not left as an afterthought. Indeed, planning the evaluation component of the program in advance can contribute to the program's design and help ensure its effectiveness. The importance of well-designed evaluation to the overall success of the program cannot be overstated.

What is important to evaluate should be discussed at the outset, subject to constraints imposed by the rules of prison administration, which can limit the feasibility of conducting experimental and quasi-experimental studies (Campbell & Stanley, 1963). Unsurprisingly, such studies have been found "virtually non-existent" among prison theater education programs (Moller, 2011, p. 11). Nevertheless, program-specific evaluations can focus on measuring the subjective experience of participants, how knowledge and skills were imparted through the program, how the program actually changed participant behavior, and/or how the outcomes advanced the institutional aims of the prison (Kirkpatrick & Kirkpatrick, 2006). Programs designed with specific, intentional outcomes can be evaluated according to how well such outcomes were achieved through the educational process (Wiggins & McTighe, 2005). As arts-in-corrections expert Grady Hillman has noted, there is no single type of successful program and each must adapt to a different environment (Hillman, 2023, p. 86), so the approach to evaluation must also be singularly designed. Much can be learned from previous evaluation studies conducted some time ago (e.g., Brewster, 1983) as well as in specific regions, such as California (e.g., Eason et al., 2021). Studies of the effects of human learning may retain validity because the human nature under study does not change appreciably and the specific methodologies of program evaluation used, including the calculation of return on investment and reducing recidivism, can be understood for the value they offer in context (Hogan, 2007).

In summary, a Carceral Creativity Framework would result in a more rationalized system for creating and disseminating works from prisons. Such a framework might also be replicable in other countries, with appropriate modifications, of course. To spur greater engagement in prison creativity, perhaps national and even international exhibits of artwork and musical performances could be arranged, with prizes in various categories, similar to PEN America's annual prison writing contest.[2]

By now I hope you might envision possible outcomes of adopting a national carceral creativity policy. Such a vision won't just happen. What we need are a few willing superintendents of creativity.

Notes

1 See: www.firststepalliance.org/, cited 30 March 2024.
2 See: https://pen.org/annual-prison-writing-contest/, cited 27 April 2024.

References

Austin, J. (2022). *Library services and incarceration: Recognizing barriers, strengthening access*. ALA and Neal Schuman.

Brewster, L. (2014). The impact of prison arts programs on inmate attitudes and behavior: A quantitative evaluation. *Justice Policy Journal, 11*(2), 28.

Brewster, L. G. (1983). *An evaluation of the arts-in-corrections program of the California Department of Corrections*. William James Association.

www.ojp.gov/ncjrs/virtual-library/abstracts/evaluation-arts-corrections-program-california-department cited 20 March 2024.

Brewster, L. G., & Merts, P. (2015). *Paths of discovery: Art practice and its impact in California prisons* (2nd ed.). Self Published.

Campbell, D. T., & Stanley, J. C. (1963). *Experimental and quasi-experimental designs for research.* Rand McNally College Publishing Company.

Davis, L. M., Bozick, R., Steele, J. L., Saunders, J., & Miles, J. N. V. (2013). *Evaluation the effectiveness of correctional education.* RAND Corporation. www.rand.org/pubs/research_reports/RR266.html cited 21 April 2024.

Eason, J. M., Haimson, C., Herelle, T., & Eason, M. (2021). *Flower grown in concrete: Exploring the healing power of the arts for people experiencing incarceration.* California Arts in Corrections. https://view.publitas.com/ca-arts-council/arts-in-corrections-2021-report/page/1 cited 22 April 2024.

Greenberger, A. (2020, July 8). Incarcerated artists are making some of today's most important art. A powerful new book explains why. *ARTnews*. www.artnews.com/art-news/artists/prison-art-nicole-fleetwood-jesse-krimes-russell-craig-tameca-cole-1202693793/ cited 5 May 2024.

Hanleybrown, F., Kania, J., & Kramer, M. R. (2012). Channeling change: Making collective impact work. *Stanford Social Innovation Review Reprint*, 8 pp.

Hillman, G. (2023). *Arts in corrections: Thirty years of annotated publications*. Routledge.

Hogan, R. L. (2007). The historical development of program evaluation: Exploring past and present. *Online Journal for Workforce Education and Development*, *2*(4, Fall), 14.

Kania, J., & Kramer, M. R. (2011). Collective impact. *Stanford Social Innovation Review* (Winter), 36–41.

Kirkpatrick, D. L., & Kirkpatrick, J. D. (2006). *Evaluating training programs: The four levels* (3rd ed.). Berrett-Koehler Publishers, Inc.

Krolak, L. (2019). *Books beyond bars: The transformative potential of prison libraries*. UNESCO Institute for Lifelong Learning. http://uil.unesco.org/adult-education/books-beyond-bars-transformative-potential-prison-libraries cited 10 February 2020.

Moller, L. (2011). Project slam: Rehabilitation through theatre at Sing Sing Correrctional Facility. *The International Journal of the Arts in Society*, *5*(5), 9–29.

Mtima, L. (2024). Copyright and the interdependent relationship between social utility and social justice. In S. D. Jamar & L. Mtima (Eds.), *The Cambridge handbook of intellectual property and social justice* (pp. 115–130). Cambridge University Press.

Mtima, L., & Whitman, J. R. (2022). Copyright protection in brief. In C. Meissner (Ed.), *The sentences that create us: Crafting a writer's life in prison*. Haymarket Books.

Whitman, J. R. (2015). An entrepreneurship approach to achieving IP social justice. In L. Mtima (Ed.), *Intellectual property, entrepreneurship and social justice: From swords to ploughshares* (pp. 33–63). Edward Elgar Publishing. https://doi.org/10.4337/9781783470259.00009

Wiggins, G., & McTighe, J. (2005). *Understanding by design* (2nd ed.). Association for Supervision and Curriculum Development.

8 Superintendents of Creativity

Returning to our introductory hypothetical, imagine that you are once again a prison superintendent. You still face daunting challenges, but you feel ready to try something new, something creative within the policy boundaries that define your role as superintendent. Perhaps you were inspired by the RTA program as featured in the film *Sing Sing*. You are mindful that 95% of those under your care could eventually be released and return home with "more education, emotional intelligence, and effective tools for healing and reducing harm," as described by Bryonn Bain in *Empowering Song: Music Education from the Margins* (de Quadros & Amrein, 2023, p. x). Maybe relations in your facility could improve.

You decide to start small, with an experiment.

After a review of free materials from PEN America, including *The Sentences That Create Us* and the companion *Writer's Workshop Curriculum Guide* (Meissner, 2022; PEN America, 2024a, 2024b), you engage a qualified arts-in-corrections consultant to explore how to set up a writing program for your residents, either as a stand-alone initiative or as part of your HobbyCraft program. Together you work out in advance the standards for evaluating the program and what success would look like. At the same time, you review your facility's library holdings in consultation with the librarian and your writing educator to make sure it is sufficiently stocked with books appropriate for learning about and inspiring writing.

As part of your plan to introduce a writing program to residents, you conduct one or more sessions with your staff and correctional officers to inform them of your experiment, to make them aware of its purpose and its potential value, including to them, and to explore how the program might contribute to their own creative interests, as well. You will need their understanding and support to succeed. As noted in journalist Bill Keller's book, *What's Prison For?*, successful reform requires the acceptance if not cooperation of correctional workers (Keller, 2022, p. 126).

Your writing program might also include a prison newsletter or anthology of works produced by residents. Perhaps this would be a way to include contributions from your staff, as well. Free materials and advice are available for this from the PJP and The Pollen Initiative. You might invite one or more outside

DOI: 10.4324/9781003566021-9

organizations that provide outlets for and dissemination of creative works to allow residents the opportunity to publish their writing on the outside. Your library should inform residents of copyright matters, including how they can protect their writing by registering for copyright protection. A protocol for registering copyrights from prison is freely available from the Copyright Alliance and Institute for Intellectual Property and Social Justice.

Rules to control inappropriate behavior, including writing about or illustrating forbidden material, would be strictly maintained. As you and your consulting educator roll out your writing program, you monitor and record how this intervention affects resident-to-resident and resident-to-officer relations and morale.

Depending on the outcomes of your writing program, you might next consider undertaking a similar experiment involving the visual arts, followed by an investment in the space and equipment to support a music studio and recording capacity. While there is no guarantee of success, and there may be setbacks, your gradual transformation of the prison to unfetter the creativity among your resident population will contribute to advancing the Intellectual Property clause of the Constitution of the United States: to benefit the nation by promoting the creative potential of all of its people.

Since you are probably *not* a prison superintendent, you can, if you are willing, encourage and support the creative impulse of people you know who are in detention, whether or not their prison offers arts-in-corrections programs. Based on what you might have learned from this book, you could be in a position to provide new hope for how an incarcerated individual can achieve the profound benefits of his or her creative talents.

In summary, unfettering the creativity of people in detention offers potential benefits to the administration of carceral facilities, to the residents who engage in creative endeavors, and to society, the nation, and the world. No reduction in mandated sentencing is required. Learning and exercising artistic skills in prison may not be for everyone, and there would be no coercion of residents to engage. But all could benefit.

Policymakers and politicians should entertain legislation and funding for new initiatives to unfetter creativity in detention. Superintendents are encouraged to contract with arts-in-corrections programs and to engage arts-in-corrections providers and other educational institutions supported by philanthropy or qualified under the Pell Grant system.[1] Friends and families of the incarcerated could provide materials to residents interested in exploring their own creative talents, subject to prison permission. Librarians could raise awareness among residents of the purpose of copyright and how to register for copyright protection. Other individuals and organizations that provide support to creators may choose to collaborate in ways to find synergies and leverage their respective strengths. Any of these actions will be helpful toward unfettering creativity across the nation at the state and federal levels.

There is no damage done by institutionalizing creativity in prison and only benefit to society, to carceral administration, and to citizens returning to the community with their dignity intact. Re-entering residents could take pride and ownership in their ability to be creative achieved through the productive use of their time while incarcerated to pay their debt to society. Regardless, incarcerated people will continue to follow their intrinsic instincts to be creative in whatever ways they can. They always have, and they always will. It's part of their human nature throughout the world, as it is in the United States.

▪ ▪ ▪

Here I would like to return to Zumar's painting on the frontispiece and suggest a different interpretation. Zumar's intent, as we know from him, was to depict a reimagining of himself as a healthier, better person while doing his time. In the act of conceiving this metaphor and then making the effort to illustrate it on canvas, Zumar exhibited extraordinary insight, determination, and skill, all intrinsically motivated. He is using the arts for self-rehabilitation. I suggest that the reimagining that Zumar exemplifies in his painting could also be applied to our society in its relationship to the penal system. A better way is possible. It may take time, experimentation, and hard work on the part of innovative carceral leaders and managers to become vocal advocates for change. But then, policymakers at the state and federal levels will have to *want* to make the necessary legislative changes to achieve our goal of a nationwide carceral creativity policy and thus achieve a more perfect and inclusive Union.

In closing, I reiterate my call for a new carceral creativity policy for the nation and hope that this work will spur progress toward adopting such an initiative. I welcome further research on the practice and societal benefit of creating expressive works in prisons in the United States and around the world to augment an evidence-based argument for transformative penal change.

Note

1 For an exemplary educational program designed for the incarcerated, see the Northwestern Prison Education Program: https://sites.northwestern.edu/npep/, cited 24 April 2024.

References

de Quadros, A., & Amrein, E. (2023). *Empowering song: Music education from the margins*. Routledge.

Keller, B. (2022). *What's prison for? Punishment and rehabilitation in the age of mass incarceration*. Columbia Global Reports.

Meissner, C. (Ed.). (2022). *The sentences that create us: Crafting a writer's life in prison*. Haymarket Books.

PEN America. (2024a). *The Freewrite Project: A writer's workshop curriculum guide*. Prison and Justice Writing, PEN America.

PEN America. (2024b). *The Freewrite Project: A writer's workshop curriculum guide, facilitator's guide*. Prison and Justice Writing, PEN America.

Appendix A
Resources

The references section at the end of each section lists all the sources cited in that section. The following are additional resources that may be of interest, though this list is far from complete.

Library of Congress

www.loc.gov/

The Library of Congress, the agency that houses the U.S. Copyright Office, offers a vast trove of materials pertaining to our subject. Using its search function, 610,227 items were listed using the term "prison literature"; 1,294,767 items for "prison art"; and 1,228,421 for "prison music." Of course, variations on these terms could be tried, as well.

Books/Chapters

If you or someone you know who is incarcerated would like to learn more about writing in prison, PEN America has produced a valuable reference book, *The Sentences That Create Us: Crafting a Writer's Life in Prison,* edited by Caits Meissner with a foreword by Reginald Dwayne Betts (Meissner, 2022). The book, specifically aimed to assist aspiring writers in prison, includes sections on different genres of literature, including poetry, fiction, drama, screenwriting, and journalism, offers views on how to write in prison, how to build a community, and provides writing exercises. Short sections on publishing and protecting copyright are also included. People in prison can order this book for free by writing to Justice Writing, c/o PEN America, 120 Broadway, 26th Floor North, New York, NY 10271.

The following books or chapters stand out as contributions to the profession and process of arts in corrections, prison librarianship, and intellectual property protection:

Paths of Discovery: Art Practice and Its Impact in California Prisons, second edition, by Larry Brewster and Peter Merts (2015)
Arts in Corrections: Thirty Years of Annotated Publications, by Grady Hillman (2023)

Regarding libraries in detention, the following books provide an outstanding overview of the history of incarceration and models of libraries serving those in detention, as well as the benefit of lifelong learning in the prison context and the role of the prison librarian, and are recommended for non-librarians as well:

Books beyond bars: The transformative potential of prison libraries, by Lisa Krolak (2019)
Library Services and Incarceration: Recognizing Barriers, Strengthening Access, by Jeanie Austin (2022)
"Intellectual Property Empowerment and Protection for Prisoners," by John R. Whitman, in *The Cambridge Handbook of Intellectual Property and Social Justice* (Whitman, 2024)
"An entrepreneurship approach to achieving IP social Justice," by John R. Whitman, in *Intellectual Property, Entrepreneurship and Social Justice* (Whitman, 2015)

Journals

American Journal of Criminal Justice
www.springer.com/journal/12103
The Howard Journal of Criminal Justice
https://onlinelibrary.wiley.com/journal/20591101
The Journal of Correctional Education
www.jstor.org/journal/jcorreduc
Journal of Prisoners on Prisons
https://uottawa.scholarsportal.info/ottawa/index.php/jpp/index
Justice Quarterly
www.tandfonline.com/journals/rjqy20

Films

View a series of short clips about how intellectual property is understood by creators in the town of Huntsville, Alabama.

https://mbiedc.org/styled-7-videos/videos.html
Watch a trailer for Master of Light, a documentary about George Anthony Morton, a classical artist with 11 years of incarceration behind him.
www.youtube.com/watch?v=9dHJGCNQBlk
Watch the trailer of a story of how residents develop an original stage production based on Rehabilitation Through the Arts.
https://youtu.be/j3dXc6P3zH8?feature=shared

Web Sites

Government Sites:

U.S. Department of Justice
Objective to Maintain a Safe and Humane Prison System
www.justice.gov/doj/doj-strategic-plan/objective-52-maintain-safe-and-humane-prison-system
U.S. Federal Bureau of Prisons
www.bop.gov/
U.S. Federal Bureau of Prisons, The First Step Act
www.bop.gov/inmates/fsa/overview.jsp
Federal Prison Oversight Act
www.ossoff.senate.gov/press-releases/signed-into-law-sens-ossoff-braun-durbin-reps-mcbath-armstrongs-bipartisan-federal-prison-oversight-act/
National Institute of Corrections, History of Corrections in America
https://nicic.gov/resources/nic-library/hot-topics/history-corrections-america
National Institute of Corrections Institutional Libraries
https://nicic.gov/tags/libraries/institutional-libraries

Nongovernmental Sites:

General:

California Lawyers for the Arts resources for arts-in-corrections
www.calawyersforthearts.org/arts-in-corrections.html
The Justice Policy Center of the Urban Institute
www.urban.org/justice-policy-center
The Marshall Project
www.themarshallproject.org/
Prison Policy Initiative
www.prisonpolicy.org/
The Sentencing Project
www.sentencingproject.org/
Women's Prison Association
www.wpaonline.org/

World Prison Brief
www.prisonstudies.org/

Literature/Writing:

The Actors' Gang Prison Project
https://theactorsgang.com/prison-project
American Prison Writing Archive
https://prisonwitness.org/
Free Minds Book Club and Writing Workshop
https://freemindsbookclub.org
PEN America Prison and Justice Writing Program
https://pen.org/prison-writing/
Pollen Initiative
https://polleninitiative.org/
Prison Journalism Project
https://prisonjournalismproject.org/
Storycatchers Theatre
www.storycatcherstheatre.org

Visual Arts:

Alabama Prison Arts and Education Project
https://apaep.auburn.edu
Art Inside
https://blog.lareviewofbooks.org/category/art-inside/
Artistic Noise
www.artisticnoise.org
California Arts in Corrections
https://artsincorrections.org
Cellblock Visions
https://cellblockvisions.com
Justice Arts Coalition
https://thejusticeartscoalition.org/
Ohio Prison Arts Connection
https://linktr.ee/ohioprisonartsconnection
Prison Arts Collective
www.prisonartscollective.com
Prison Arts Resource Project
https://scancorrectionalarts.org/about-scan/
Prison Photography
https://prisonphotography.org/
Project Youth ArtReach
www.goartivate.org/about-pya/

Rehabilitation Through the Arts
www.rta-arts.org
William James Association, Prison Arts Project
https://williamjamesassociation.org/prison-arts-project/

Music:

Die Jim Crow, see FREER Records
www.diejimcrow.com/
FREER Records
www.freerrecords.com/
How one Boston University researcher is empowering prisoners with music
www.bu.edu/articles/2020/how-one-bu-researcher-is-empowering-prisoners-with-music/
Jail Guitar Doors
www.jailguitardoors.org
Musicambia
www.musicambia.org
Righteous Babe Prison Music Project
www.righteousbabe.com/pages/prisonmusicproject
Songs in the Key of Free
www.songsinthekeyoffree.com
What no one tells you about recording music in prison
https://ennuimagazine.com/recording-music-in-prison/
Zeo Boekbinder's Prison Music Project
http://zeoboekbinder.com/prisonmusicproject

Libraries:

ALA expanding information access for incarcerated people
www.ala.org/aboutala/offices/diversity/expanding-access-incarcerated-initiative
ALA library services to the incarcerated and detained
www.ala.org/asgcla/interestgroups/iglsid
ALA library services to the justice involved
www.ala.org/advocacy/diversity/services-incarcerated
IFLA Prison Libraries Working Group
https://mail.iflalists.org/wws/info/prison-l
Prison-l listserv
www.cvl-lists.org/mailman3/postorius/lists/prison-l@cvl-lists.org/
San Francisco Public Library jail and re-entry services
https://sfpl.org/services/jail-and-reentry-services
State prison libraries directory
https://washstatelib.libguides.com/directoryofstateprisonlibraries/home

Social Justice:

Equal Justice Initiative
https://eji.org/
Institute for Intellectual Property and Social Justice
https://iipsj.org/
Museum for Black Innovation and Entrepreneurship
https://mbiedc.org/
Southern Center for Human Rights
www.schr.org/who-we-are/history/
Vera Institute of Justice
www.vera.org/

Associations:

American Correctional Association
www.aca.org
Correctional Education Association
https://ceanational.org

International:

European Prison Education Association (EPEA)
www.epea.org/
European Society of Criminology
https://esc-eurocrim.org/v2/
National Criminal Justice Arts Alliance (UK)
https://artsincriminaljustice.org.uk
Penal Reform International
www.penalreform.org/
World Prison Brief
www.prisonstudies.org/

Other:

Bard Prison Initiative
https://bpi.bard.edu
Copyright Alliance
https://copyrightalliance.org
Prison Public Memory Project
www.prisonpublicmemory.org
Prison Research and Innovation Initiative
www.urban.org/projects/prison-research-and-innovation-initiative-prii
Center for Law, Brain, and Behavior Neurolaw Library
https://clbbneurolawlibrary.com/

Appendix B
Methodology

In my research for this book, I sought to compile primary source, first person accounts of creativity in prison, stories of individuals currently engaged in creative work who could exemplify the promise of a new creative carceral policy.

To identify individuals, I requested nominations from the Justice Arts Coalition, PEN America, FREER Records, John J. Lennon (a renowned prison journalist), and the American Prison Writing Archive, which declined due to its policy to protect its contributors. I also invited three artists whose works, created while in detention, are in my personal collection. One did not respond. Finally, I consulted the *Art for Justice Fund Directory* of previously supported artists from 2017 to 2023, and emailed nine formerly incarcerated artists, one of whom responded.

Following general guidelines for the protection of human subjects in research, I prepared a cover letter, permission form, and questionnaire, and in early December 2023 requested an assessment of face validity of these materials from several experts, including Professor André de Quadros, a human rights activist and professor of music at Boston University; Prison Writing Program Manager Robert Pollock at PEN America, arts-in-corrections expert and teacher Grady Hillman, prison writing professor Doran Larson, and formerly incarcerated writer, R. Dwayne Betts. All but Mr. Betts responded and indicated approval of the materials. Mr. Pollock made several constructive suggestions for changes, which I adopted. The final versions of these instruments are available on request.

Beginning in mid-January 2024, I sent letters consisting of these instruments through the postal service to nominated and selected individuals residing in detention. One prison blocked my correspondence to two residents despite following their recommended guidelines, and in one case, correspondence from a prison resident in Ohio was lost in the postal service. Once I assembled responses, drawing as well from other notes and correspondence with individuals, I prepared short notes about each, paraphrasing or quoting their accounts. I sent each individual the relevant portion to review, correct, amend, and approve prior to publication. Some asked that I use their pseudonyms.

I compensated each respondent with a $50 honorarium for participating, an additional $20 for each piece of artwork reproduced in the book, and $10 for each link to a music recording. The results represent individual cases from a non-random, convenience sample and do not provide a statistical basis for extrapolation to other prison residents. I am responsible for any errors or omissions in recounting these stories.

Index

For Product Safety Concerns and Information please contact our EU representative GPSR@taylorandfrancis.com
Taylor & Francis Verlag GmbH, Kaufingerstraße 24, 80331 München, Germany

www.ingramcontent.com/pod-product-compliance
Lightning Source LLC
LaVergne TN
LVHW010920110826
845149LV00013B/2431
* 9 7 8 1 0 3 2 9 3 4 7 7 8 *